DISCIP

THE NATIONS

By the same author:

The Christian Philosophy of Education Explained, 1992
Christianity and Law, 1993
The Nature, Government and Function of the Church, 1997
A Defence of the Christian State, 1998
The Political Economy of a Christian Society, 2001
Common-Law Wives and Concubines, 2003
The Problem of the "Gifted Speaker," 2009
Baal Worship Ancient and Modern, 2010
The Great Decommission, 2011
The Christian Passover: Agape Feast or Ritual Abuse? 2012
The Politics of God and the Politics of Man, 2016

DISCIPLE THE NATIONS

STEPHEN C. PERKS

KUYPER FOUNDATION
TAUNTON • ENGLAND
2022

Published in Great Britain by
THE KUYPER FOUNDATION
P. O. Box 2, Taunton, Somerset,
TA1 4ZD, England

ISBN 978-1-909145-03-0

British Library Cataloguing-in-Publication Data
A catalogue record for this book is available
from the British Library

Printed and bound in Great Britain

PREFACE

This book has its origin in a talk I gave to a group of twenty-four people in late July 2021. The talk consisted of a slightly shorter version of Part Two of this book, "How to Disciple the Nations." All the material in Part One was made available to the group as preparatory reading before the meeting took place and had been previously published online as short articles. The purpose of the talk and the meeting following it was to stimulate discussion about how to create an apostolic community that can act as a catalyst around which a wider local Christian community can develop and from which missionaries can go out to found other apostolic communities that will reproduce in the same way. The purpose of this vision of apostolic mission and Christian community is the seeking of the Kingdom of God and the fulfilment of the Great Commission,—i.e. the discipling of the nations—and this remains the purpose of this book.

The most important part of this book is Part Two, §5 "How to create Christian communities: Apostolic Foundations." Everything else in the argument of Part Two leads up to this. But in order to understand my argument in context here it is important to read what comes before it. Likewise, the argument of Part Two presupposes the reading of the preparatory material in Part One of this book.

There is some overlap of material in the articles that comprise Part One since they were originally published as a series of individual short articles. Because they were originally published separately the articles in Part One may at first seem somewhat disconnected, but each article deals with an aspect of Church life that is highly problematic and needs to be addressed decisively if we are to move on in the way that the argument of Part Two proposes. Therefore in order to get the best out of Part Two the material in Part One should be read first.

I should like to express my thanks to Randy Sperger, Lester Gonzalez and Jason Lawton, with whom I have spent many hours discussing the material in Part Two §5, "How to create Christian communities: Apostolic Foundations," and which has been very helpful in bringing my understanding of this subject into greater focus, thereby enabling me to see and articulate the issues involved with much greater clarity. I should also like to thank Scott Tucker, Yavor Rusinov, Mark Kreitzer and Jordan Wilson for reading earlier drafts of the book and providing me with some critical feedback and encouragement.

STEPHEN C. PERKS
November, 2021

TABLE OF CONTENTS

DEFINITION OF TERMS

§1
Church (*kyrikon*)

There are problems with the use of the English word *church*. We use the word in a variety of ways to mean different things, usually without defining what we mean by it and very often without even being aware ourselves that we are using the same term in different ways to refer to different things. This leads to confused thinking and consequently to misunderstanding. In order to avoid these problems we need to understand something of the etymology and history of the word and its use, and we need to be careful in our use of the term to make sure that we understand ourselves and indicate clearly to others what we mean by it.

The English word *church* comes from the Old English *cirice* or *circe*, which is derived from the Greek word *kyrikon*, meaning *God's house*, a popular fourth-century form of the Greek word *kyriakon*, an adjective meaning *imperial*, *of the lord*. This Greek word was used of "the Lord's house" (*to kyriakon doma*).[1] The English word *church* is derived, via this route, from the Greek adjective *kyriakos*.[2] This adjective is used only twice in the New Testament, however, and in neither instance does it have reference to the Greek word *ecclesia*, which is the word usually translated as *church* in English translations of the Bible. In 1 Cor. 11:20 it is used of the *Lord's*

[1] The German word for church, *kirche*, shares the same etymology. Compare, however, the French, *église*, the Spanish, *iglesia*, and the Italian, *chiesa*, which are all derived from the Greek word *ecclesia*.

[2] H. D. Liddell and R. Scott, *A Greek-English Lexicon* (Oxford: The Clarendon Press, 1901), p. 862*a*; Gerhard Kittel and Gerhard Friedrich, eds, *Theological Dictionary of the New Testament* (Grand Rapids, Michigan: Wm B. Eerdmans Publishing Company, 1965), Vol. III, p. 532 n. 92.

Supper, and in Rev. 1:10 it is used of the *Lord's day*. Nowhere in the New Testament is this term used to refer to the *Lord's house*. Strictly speaking therefore, the notion or concept of the *church* is not part of the new covenant—though it is of course part of the old covenant, i.e. the Temple. The concept of the church—i.e. a building and its appurtenances, set apart as a special sanctuary for Christian worship—is not found in the New Testament and is not a feature of the new covenant.

In his translation of the New Testament William Tyndale did not use the word *church* to translate the Greek word *ecclesia* and rendered it more accurately throughout as *congregation*. Nowhere in Tyndale's translation of the New Testament do we find the word *church* used of the assembly or community of believers.[3] The New Testament does not identify the *ecclesia* as the house of the Lord, i.e. a building and its appurtenances, but as the people of God, a covenant community called out of the world of sin and unbelief into fellowship with God as his holy *nation* (1 Pet. 2:9). Unfortunately, subsequent translations of the Bible into English, including the Geneva Bible, did not follow Tyndale's lead in this matter and mistranslated the Greek word *ecclesia* as *church*.

The English word *church* is used in most English translations of the Bible to translate the Greek word *ecclesia*. This is a mistranslation since the *ecclesia* is not a building but an assembly of the people constituted as a body politic (see §2 "Assembly" below). There were, strictly speaking therefore, no Christian churches in the New Testament; believers met in their homes or in other places, but there were no specially designated buildings set apart for Christian worship. There was the Temple of course, and there were synagogues, where the first Jewish Christians probably worshipped on the sabbath, but they were soon obliged to leave these, and they worshipped elsewhere on the Lord's day, the day after the Jewish Sabbath, and Gentile Christians never worshipped in the

[3] At Acts 19:37, for example, he uses the word *churches*, but the Greek word that he is translating is *hierosylous*, i.e. *robbers of temples*, *sacrilegious persons*, not *ecclesia*, and refers to a building and its appurtenances, not the assembly of the Christian community.

synagogues. Originally, however, the term *synagogue* did not refer to a building either, but to a gathering of people, an assembly (from the Greek word *synago*, meaning *to gather together*), and was used of local communities of Jews who met together on the sabbath for worship, instruction in the law and for educational and social purposes. That is to say, it referred to people, a community, not to a building, and only came to signify a building at a later date because of its use as a metonym for the building in which the community met. It was exactly the opposite with the term *church*; that is to say, the building, which is properly called a *church* from the etymological point of view, came to signify the community of Christians that met in it.

According to *The Concise Oxford Dictionary of Current English* (Eighth Edition, 1990) the English word *church* can mean: 1. a building for public worship, 2. a meeting for public worship in such a building; then, with the first letter capitalised (Church), 3. the body of all Christians, 4. the clergy or clerical profession, 5. an organised Christian group or society of any time, country, or distinct principles of worship, 6. institutionalised religion as a political or social force.

In this book I use the word *Church*, with the first letter capitalised, to refer to what is predominantly understood by the term in common usage, i.e. the liturgical institution with its rituals, discipline and bureaucracy governed by clergymen (not all modern denominations use the term *clergyman*, but the concept to which the word refers is endemic in all of them).

§2
Assembly (*ecclesia*)

The correct translation of the Greek word *ecclesia* is *assembly* not *church*. The word *ecclesia*, which is usually and incorrectly translated as *church* in most English versions of the Bible, is derived from a Greek verb (*eccaleo*) meaning *to call out* or *summon forth*.[4] The noun,

[4] Liddel and Scott, *op. cit.*, p. 434*b*.

ecclesia, is a *political* term meaning *an assembly of the citizens regularly summoned, the legislative assembly.*[5] The *ecclesia* was, from the fifth century B.C., the assembly of the *demos* in Athens and most Greek city States,[6] the *demos* being the classical Greek term for "the people as organized into a body politic."[7] In its use of the term *ecclesia*, therefore, the New Testament stresses not only that members of the body of Christ are called *out of* the world of sin and unbelief, but also that they are called *into* participation in a new *political* organism, a new community or society, with its own distinctive social order: the Kingdom of God. The members of the Lord Jesus Christ's assembly, his *ecclesia*, constitute a holy *nation* under one Lord who is sovereign over the whole of life. In claiming Christ as Lord, therefore, Christians declare allegiance to a new King whose jurisdiction is total and whose law is to govern all human thoughts, actions and relationships with all other people and things.

The word *ecclesia* is a *political* term not a *cultic* term; i.e. it is not a term denoting the meeting of a group of people united by their devotion to a particular deity and the maintenance and promotion of his cultus. There were many words available to denote such cultic groups in classical Greek culture and literature, which the authors of the New Testament could have used to identify the assembly of Christians primarily as a cultic group devoted to maintaining the cult of Jesus. But the New Testament, written by men under the inspiration of the Holy Spirit, does not use such words of the assemblies of Christians. The New Testament does not identify the *ecclesia*, the assembly of those who serve the Lord Jesus Christ, as a mystery cult, but as the assembly of the citizens of a new *political* order, the Kingdom of God, and the purpose of their assembling together is to equip the members of the assembly in their calling to proclaim in word and deed the good news of the Kingdom of God to the whole world, until all the *nations* of the earth have submitted to the Lord Jesus Christ as his disciples.

[5] *Ibid.*, p. 435*a*.
[6] Gerhard Kittel and Gerhard Friedhrich, *op. cit.*, Vol. III, p 513.
[7] J. H. Thayer, *A Greek-English Lexicon of the New Testament* (Edinburgh: T. and T. Clark, 1901), p. 132.

§3
NATION (*ethnos*)

The Greek word *ethnos*, which is translated as *nation* in English Bibles means, according to Abbot-Smith, "1. *a multitude, a company*, whether of beasts or men (Hom.). 2. *a nation, people* . . . 3. In pl. as in the O[old] T[estament] . . . *the nations*, as distinct from Israel, *Gentiles*."[8] According to Liddell and Scott it means "*a number of people living together, a company, body of men* . . . *a band* of comrades . . . *a host* of men . . . and of particular tribes . . . and of animals . . . *swarms, flocks* etc. 2. After Hom., *a nation, people* . . . in the N.T. and Eccl. . . . *the nations, Gentiles*, i.e. all except Jews and Christians . . . 3. *a particular class* of men, *a caste, tribe*."[9] According to Kittel's *Theological Dictionary of the New Testament* it means " 'a mass' or 'host' or 'multitude' bound by the same manners, customs or other distinctive features. Applied to men it gives us the sense of people; but it can be used of animals in the sense of 'herd' or of insects in the sense of 'swarm' . . . In most cases [*ethnos*] is used of men in the sense of a 'people.' " Compared with other words such as *laos* ("people as a political unity with a common history and constitution") and *glossa* ("people as a linguistic unity") *ethnos* "is the most general and therefore the weakest of these terms, having simply an ethnographical sense and denoting the natural cohesion of a people in general."[10] *Ethnos* does not mean *State*. It is a much broader and wider concept than merely the State. Of interest also is the statement in Kittel's *Theological Dictionary of the New Testament* that the word *ethnos* probably comes from the Greek word *ethos*, which means *habit, use, custom, cultic ordinance, law*.[11] An *ethnos*, a nation, in this sense means a company of men bound by the same customs, laws, cultic ordinances, habits etc.

[8] G. Abbott-Smith, *A Manual Greek Lexicon of the New Testament* (Edinburgh: T. & T. Clark, 1986), p. 129.

[9] Liddel and Scott, *op. cit*, p. 412*a*.

[10] Gerhard Kittel and Gerhard Friedrich, *op. cit.*, Vol. II, p. 369.

[11] *Ibid.*, 372f.

It is clear from this why the New Testament, although it never refers to the body of Christ, the Christian community, as a *church* (*kyrikon*) but rather primarily as an *assembly* (*ecclesia*), also refers to the body of Christ as a *nation* (*ethnos*, 1 Pet. 2:9) and addresses the nation of Christ with the same words that Moses addressed the nation of Israel in Ex. 19:6 (cf. Lev. 20:26; Dt. 7:6; Rev. 1:6, 5:10).

PROLOGUE

On the eve of the Reformation the Roman Catholic Church was a bath with two very dirty babies in it. One was doctrine and the other was works. Both were so dirty they were almost unrecognisable. The Reformers recognised the doctrine baby and saved it, but failed to see the works baby and threw it out with the dirty bath water. Well within a century of the English Reformation and the dissolution of the monasteries the government was passing poor laws to help those who were no longer being cared for by the monastic system. Of course this is a complex subject and I am painting with a very broad brush. A detailed examination of this subject will reveal its complexities. I am not claiming that the Reformers had no works at all any more than the Roman Catholics had no doctrine. The real issue is one's understanding of the nature of both doctrine and works. Nevertheless, the fact that one of the long-term consequences of the Reformation was that care of the poor and sick passed from the Church, however badly administered, to the State, under which it has been even more badly administered and with portentous prospects for the future of Western civilisation socially and politically, is a prodigious indication of the problem. Our modern social dilemma, and the rise of socialism and the Welfare State, which is secular humanism's defective and ungodly answer to that dilemma, is the consequence of a half-cocked Reformation.

Moreover, there were two Reformations, not one: the Magisterial and the Radical. The Magisterial Reformation ultimately failed and gave way to the Radical Reformation, which has now triumphed in the Protestant world, thereby corrupting almost beyond recognition the doctrine that the Magisterial Reformation saved from the dirty bath water of the Roman Catholic Church.

As a consequence, Protestantism, like Roman Catholicism, is now over.

It has taken 500 years for the full implications of this defective half-cocked Reformation to become manifest and its inadequacy clearly understood, though most Protestants even now fail to recognise the truth staring them in the face. As always, the real answer to this dilemma lies with a full-scale renaissance of the Christian faith, not another half-cocked Reformation, which will achieve nothing. The purpose of this book is to propose a way forward to the realisation of that full-scale renaissance of the Christian faith.

PART ONE

PREPARATORY READING

§1

Christian Renaissance

Why there never was a Reformation

We use the term all the time and we speak endlessly of the theology that created it and that then flowed from it as if it actually existed and accomplished something. But it is a fantasy. There never was a Reformation, there are no Reformed Churches, and Reformed theology is a fiction. This misnomer is now a deadly trap that those who wish to pursue the Kingdom of God must recognise as such if they wish to avoid another forty years in the wilderness.

Well, you may think I am about to jump ship and become a Roman Catholic, but nothing could be further from the truth. My point is that the Roman Church was not reformed, and has never been reformed. It is true that due to the rise of nation States it has less power today than it had in the sixteenth century, but it is just as corrupt doctrinally and morally today as it was in the sixteenth century, indeed even more corrupt in some ways. What we call the Reformation was not a Reformation at all. It was an Exodus. The Reformers never reformed the Roman Church. Not one Reformer achieved such a reformation. And if one had, Protestants would not recognise him as a Reformer at all. Misuse of words and terms can be a great snare. The Reformers did not reform any Church. If they had done so there would exist today a Reformed Roman Catholic Church. No such Church exists. Rather, they left the Roman Church, or were thrown out of it, and they then started again. They built a new Church altogether.

The correct term for what the Reformers accomplished is *Ecclesial Renaissance*, i.e. a *new birth* of the Church. They did not reform the Church, they *left* the Roman Catholic Church and their work led to the rebirth of the Christian Church in a new form. Unfortunately the word *renaissance* is used for the Humanist Renaissance that preceded what we call the Reformation and so its use to describe the work of the Reformers is likely to cause confusion, although in some respects the Reformation was part of the Renaissance, and in other respects not so. Nevertheless, the term *Ecclesial Renaissance* is the correct description of the great work that the Reformers accomplished.

Now, you may well say that it was not the Church that the Reformers were trying to reform but the Christian faith, and therefore the word *Reformation* is the correct term. That would in principle be a valid argument if it were true, and then the word *Reformation* would be used properly. But that was not the case, although it was certainly the case that the Reformers did reform the doctrine that had become so highly corrupted under the Roman Catholic magisterium, and this was a great and necessary work, though not the only work needed. Nevertheless, it was the *Church* that the Reformers set out to reform. But this was a failure, and it was a *complete* failure. What they did was to abandon the old wineskin. The existence of many people who desired to reform the Church prior to the Reformation shows that the Christian faith was alive and well. The problem was the wineskin, not the wine, and it was the wineskin that the Reformers abandoned because they were unable to reform it.

In this they were following the teaching of Jesus, whether they recognised it or not. The wineskin had become useless. Certainly the Reformers wanted Reformation, they wanted to reform the *Church* of Rome, but that is not what God gave them. New wineskins were needed. I am not denying of course that the Reformers did a great and necessary work. They did. What I am saying is that the mistaken idea that they reformed the Church has led us astray into the belief that we must reform the modern apostate Protestant Church. But Reformation is not the answer. The Protestant Church is unreformable, not because God cannot reform an apostate Church—of course he can—but because God does not reform apostate Churches. If the salt has lost its saltiness it is fit for what? To be reformed? No! It is fit for *nothing* except to be *thrown out*. I did not say this. The Lord Jesus Christ said it, just as he said that old wineskins are useless in holding the new wine and that new wineskins are necessary. And it appears now that God has thrown out the Protestant Church wineskin, which is salt that has lost its saltiness.

Do not take my word for it. Look at history. Which Churches, once they had lost their saltiness, once they had become useless and were no more than cracked old wineskins, once they were *apostate*, has God ever reformed? Not the Greek Orthodox Church. Not the Nestorian Church—which, incidentally, was in the early centuries of the Christian era one of the greatest missionary Churches that the world has ever seen, but by the time of Kubilai Kahn was utterly useless to Kubilai in his desire to Christianise his empire. Not the Roman Church or Orthodox Russian Church, nor the Coptic Church. Which Churches, and when, did God ever reform once this level of corruption and apostasy had set in? None that I know of. Maybe God has reformed one and I am just displaying my ignorance. If so, please tell me which and I shall join immediately. Please disabuse me of my ignorance. Ignorance is of no use to me. Please put me out of my misery. Nothing would please me more or be of greater relief to me in my calling. I have looked for such a Church for many years. I am not talking about finding a perfect Church so please do not quote that hackneyed and useless old phrase about never finding a perfect Church—it is the feeble mantra of every tin-pot pope that is desperate to hold on to his idolatrous tyranny. Such statements are sheer stupidity and if they had any value they would render the work of the Reformers useless. Remember, I am not denying that the work that the Reformers did was necessary and vital. It was, although it was not sufficient or complete in and of itself. What I am denying is that it was a Reformation of the Church.

It seems incontestable to me now that although God can reform apostate Churches he does not do so. God has never reformed an apostate Church. "If the salt has lost its saltiness, how can it be made salty again? It is no longer good for anything, except to be *reformed*." Is that what Jesus really said? Of course not. He said: "If the salt has lost its saltiness, how can it be made salty again?"—in other words it cannot be made salty again—"It is no longer good for *anything*, except to be *thrown out and trampled underfoot*" (Mt. 5:13). Either we believe the words of the Lord Jesus or we do not. God does not reform apostate Churches. He starts again. The new wine *must* have new wineskins if it is not to be wasted. Not only the Bible but history as well teaches this lesson. The Protestant Church has gone the way of the rest and is unreformable because God does not reform apostate Churches.

The Reformation was not a Reformation of anything. It was an *Exodus* and a *new beginning*, a *rebirth* of the Church. We do not need any more Reformations. They are useless because God does not deal in Church Reformations, he deals in new beginnings, new births, renaissance, *resurrection*—but of course there can be no resurrection without the death of what went before. We need an Exodus and a new beginning, a Christian *renaissance*. But this *renaissance* needs to be much wider and more exhaustive than a mere *ecclesial* renaissance. It must be nothing less than *resurrection*, the birth of a new Christian social order, a new Christian *civilisation*.

Of course, I am not interested in arguing about mere words. I have used the term *Reformation* all my Christian life. But I must now reform my thinking about this according to God's word (I am speaking here of reforming my *thinking*, not the *Church*—God does reform *individuals*, but even that is a new beginning, a new birth: "if anyone is in Christ he is a new creation; old things have passed away; behold, all things have become new"—2 Cor. 5:17. But the point is that God does not reform *Churches*). The problem here is that words and terms can and do mislead us. Ill-considered language can lead us astray in our understanding. We must therefore subject our minds, our very thinking process, to the word of God so that we think properly. Scripture tells us that the Holy Spirit works through the renewing of the *mind.* We must therefore be disciplined in our thinking according to what Scripture teaches. And Scripture does not teach Reformation. It teaches Exodus and resurrection. There have been *no* Reformations in the history of the Church, only Exoduses and resurrections, new beginnings.

But there is an even greater danger waiting for us here than merely being led astray in our language and thinking, namely, that at least for a great many Christians the real reason they refuse to leave Egypt is that they have made an idol out of it and they prefer idolatry to liberty, because as John Owen so aptly put it, the Church is the greatest idol that ever was in the world.[12]

The Reformation never happened. The Reformers wanted it, desperately, but they did not get it. They asked God for a stone, but he gave them bread instead (Mt. 7:9). "If ye then, being evil, know how to give good gifts unto your children, how much more shall your Father which is in heaven give good things to them that ask him?" (Mt. 7:11). We need an Exodus and renaissance, not a Reformation, and we need to pray for an Exodus and renaissance not a Reformation, because God will not give us a Reformation and we need to pray according to Scripture and God's will.

But here is the important point: in our generation there has never been a better time to start on this new beginning, this Exodus and conquest of the promised land, than the present, since these dreadful Churches, these temples of heresy and apostasy, have now shown themselves to be utterly compromised with the world and complicit with the godless secular State in its fascist aspirations to replace God as sovereign over every aspect of human life. The Church has not merely been silent, but complicit with this diabolical agenda. The time has surely come for Christians to gird up their loins, start on a new Exodus into the promised land, and reclaim their citizenship of the Kingdom of God from those who have sought to dispossess them of it for so long. Reform will not take us where we need to be and should be. It will merely trap us in

[12] John Owen, *An Inquiry into the Original, Nature, Institution, Powers, Order, and Communion of Evangelical Churches* in *Works* (Edinburgh: The Banner of Truth Trust [Goold Edition, 1850–53], 1965), Vol. XV, p. 224f.

the past, a past that will repeat the paralysis, cowardice and failure that characterised the Church in the twentieth century. We must leave Egypt, leave the house of slavery, and pursue the freedom under God that the Lord Jesus Christ has promised us.

There is no doubt plenty in this article that you can wilfully misrepresent wildly and shoot me down in flames for. By all means enjoy yourself, I have come to expect nothing less. But remember, when all the argy-bargy is over you will still be in an unreformable Church with only one *biblical* and *historically proven* way out, and you will still be faced with the same choice: either idolatry or Exodus. The Kingdom of God cannot be reached through the Reformation of apostate Churches. It can be reached only through Exodus and conquest, new birth, renaissance, *resurrection*. We are not called to reform Egypt (the corrupt and apostate Church structures of the past), but to conquer the promised land (i.e. disciple the nations). When we do that, and when we seek the Kingdom of God and his righteousness above all else, the nations of the earth shall come to us and say: "Teach us the way of the Lord" (Isaiah 2:1–4), and all the nations will become the disciples of the Lord Jesus Christ (Mt. 28:19 cf. Rev. 11:15).

§2
CHURCH PLANTING—TOTALLY COCKEYED!
A vision God never gave us for a job he never gave us

Jesus never told us to plant Churches. He said *he* will build his *ecclesia*, his assembly. He told *us* to seek the *Kingdom of God* and his *righteousness* (i.e. *justice*, not piety) and in the Great Commission he gave us a command to disciple *nations*, not plant Churches. Assemblies of Christians are a consequence of the Great Commission not its goal. The goal is all *nations* embracing the Kingdom of God and living according to the covenant. For nigh on two thousand years Christians, at the behest of self-appointed clergymen, which are nowhere to be found in the New Testament assemblies, have been reversing this order, insisting that we should do Jesus' job and that he should do ours. Is there any wonder that the Church across the board is in such a dysfunctional and paralysed state? We should do what Jesus commanded us to do and let him do what he promised he would do. Our first priority is the Kingdom of God and Christian *nations*, not Churches, and until we stop idolising the Church, which John Owen so aptly described as the greatest idol that ever was in the world, and obey the Lord Jesus' command to disciple *nations* things will continue to go wrong, as they are so evidently doing now.

Of course these Churches are not what the New Testament means when it talks about the *ecclesia*. The institutional Churches are networks of mere Christian mystery cults, not communities of God's people living as a Christian social order and discipling the nations by modelling to the world what true society should be. The word *ecclesia* is a political term, not a cultic term. There were words that could have been used in the first century to describe the meetings of Christians as essentially devotional mystery cults, which is what the Churches are today. But the Bible avoids these terms like the plague, and uses instead an intensely *political* term that was guaranteed to provoke the Roman political authorities like a red rag to a bull. The *ecclesia* is the assembly of the *demos* (the people) for *political* purposes, in other words the parliament of another political order, the Kingdom of God.

The Church has become a second rate alternative to the Kingdom of God, and Church planting has become a third rate alternative to the Great Commission to make Christian *nations*. Jesus never commanded us to make disciples of all nations. He commanded us to make all nations his disciples.

All men and nations must and one day will bow the knee to Jesus Christ and acknowledge him as the ruler of all nations. Our job, our Great Commission, is to seek and work for this now on earth. The Lord Jesus Christ will not return until all nations have submitted to him and this vision has become the reality of life on earth.

"Go therefore and make all the nations my disciples [i.e. disciple all the nations], baptizing them [i.e. all the nations] in the name of the Father and of the Son and of the Holy Spirit, teaching them [i.e. all the nations] to observe all things that I have commanded you" (Mt. 28:18-20). "And the seventh angel sounded; and there were great voices in heaven, saying, The kingdoms of *this* world are become the kingdoms of our Lord, and of his Christ; and he shall reign for ever and ever" (Rev. 11:15). This is the alpha and omega of eschatology.

§3
THE WRONG PRIORITY
Christianity: Cult or Kingdom?

"Walk ye not in the statutes of your fathers, neither observe their judgements, neither defile yourselves with their idols: I am the Lord your God; walk in my statutes, and keep my judgements, and do them" (Ezek. 20:18–19).

The chief and greatest error of the Christian Church throughout the two thousand years of her history has been to have had the wrong priority and to have made this erroneous priority the touchstone of orthodoxy. This error has existed in all branches and denominations; it continues to this day and the Church world-wide shows little if any sign that she understands the problem let alone that she is prepared to repent of the idolatry that is at the heart of it. Yet the results of this error have been catastrophic for the pursuit of the Great Commission.

The Church has told us almost universally and almost continually that the rituals, worship services and prayer meetings of the institutional Church are the essence of the Christian faith, the most important aspect of the Christian life, the most spiritual activity that the Christian can engage in, and that therefore these activities constitute the highest and purest form of worship that the Christian can offer to God and consequently that they are the most important thing in life that he can do. It is this nucleus of activities that constitutes the Church's highest priority and therefore the *Christian's* highest priority, and it is this nucleus of activities that defines worship (where worship is understood as taking place in other contexts it is only because such worship takes a similar form, as a sort of satellite Church service that mimics the form of the regular services held in Church buildings). This has been the priority that the Church has put first historically; and so great has been this emphasis, this idolatry, that we have been told repeatedly, and not only by the Roman Catholic Church, but by Protestants as well, that there can be no salvation outside of this formal organisation of the Church as an institutional cult with its rituals, government and discipline. And so, although the statement is not biblical, it has been claimed repeatedly that "He can no longer have God as his Father who does not have the Church for his mother."[13]

But the truth is that this emphasis and priority has reduced the Christian religion to little more than a Christian mystery cult, i.e. a personal salvation cult. To be saved one must join the cult and engage in the re-enactment of the mysteries through performance of the correct rituals. This may appear more obvious in the Roman Catholic, Orthodox and other Episcopal Churches, but it is not essentially any different in the Protestant Churches. The Roman Churches perform the Mass each Sunday, which is an attempt to re-enact in ritual form the sacrifice of Christ. The Anglican Churches celebrate the Eucharist each Sunday, which is more or less, depending on what kind of Anglican Church it is, Anglo-Catholic or Low Church, a dumbed-down version of the Mass. The Pentecostal and Charismatic Churches attempt to re-enact the day of Pentecost each Sunday morning. The Reformed and Presbyterian Churches try to re-enact Reformed preaching

[13] This is not a biblical doctrine. The statement goes back at least to Cyprian, a third century bishop of Carthage and martyr (*On the Unity of the Church*, para. 6, in *The Ante-Nicene Fathers* [Edinburgh: T. and T. Clark/Grand Rapids, Michigan: Wm B. Eerdmans Publishing Company, trans. Ernest Wallis], Vol. V, p. 423*a*), but it has been repeated many times since both by Roman Catholics and Protestants and has become a widely accepted yet unintelligible mantra of the Church. The real purpose of this doctrine throughout history has been to justify the excessive ecclesiastical authority that clergymen claim for themselves but have difficulty justifying in any other way.

and the worship services of the Reformation. In all these Churches the faith is reduced to a re-enactment cult. The rituals vary but not the perspective, i.e. that what the congregation does on a Sunday morning in the Church service constitutes the essence of the Christian faith and therefore the highest priority of the Christian life. The Christian faith is deemed to be not essentially about a *life* of service, i.e. obedience to God in the whole of life, but rather about making sure the right rituals are performed in the Church meeting.

But is this biblical? Is this what the Lord Jesus Christ taught? Is it what the New Testament teaches? Emphatically not! There is nothing in the Bible that supports this perversion of the gospel. What then is the biblical priority? Jesus came preaching the *Kingdom of God* (Mk 1:14), and he told us clearly what our priority should be: "seek ye first the *kingdom of God* and his *righteousness*" (Mt. 6:33). The Lord Jesus Christ does not often refer to the *ecclesia* and never to the rituals and forms of worship that have come to define the life of the Church.[14] Neither does the New Testament stress this idolatrous priority. It is the invention of clergymen, whose chief priority has always been to put themselves and their own ecclesiastical work first, *not* the Kingdom of God.

Let's take a test case. The disciples asked Jesus how to pray. His answer was what we call the Lord's prayer (Mt. 6:9–13). We may confidently take it that this prayer teaches us clearly what the Lord's priorities are in prayer, and here they are,—*this* is what Jesus commands us to pray for: *first*, that God's name should be honoured; *second*, that we should seek the coming of the Kingdom of God; *third*, that we should ask for our needs to be met; *fourth*, that we should seek forgiveness for our sins and forgive others their sins in like manner; *fifth*, that we might not face temptation and be delivered from evil; and *sixth*, an affirmation that the Kingdom,

[14] He did of course institute the Lord's Supper, but the Church abandoned Christ's ordinance in the early centuries of the Church's history and substituted for it a ritualistic and cultic reinterpretation of her own devising. See my book *The Christian Passover: Agape Feast or Ritual Abuse* (Taunton: Kuyper Foundation, 2012). A free PDF of the text can be downloaded at: www.kuyper.org/books.

power and glory belong to God. We are not even commanded to pray for the Church here, but for the *coming of the Kingdom*. Always, Jesus and the New Testament prioritise the *Kingdom of God*, not the Church. "Let us make sure" says V. H. Stanton "that we realise the extraordinarily prominent position which the subject of the Kingdom of God occupies in the Gospels, more especially in the Synoptics. This is *essential* if we would form a *true conception* of the nature of Christianity . . . descriptions of the characteristics of the Kingdom, expositions of its laws, accounts of the way men were actually receiving it, forecasts of its future, make up the whole central portion of the synoptic narrative."[15] In short, "In our Lord's teaching the Kingdom of God is the representative and all-embracing summary of his distinctive mission."[16]

It is men who have made the Christian faith *Church*-centred, not the Lord Jesus Christ, and not the Bible. The consequence of this has been a truncated, cut-down, version of the gospel, which should be the good news of the *Kingdom of God* (Mk 1:14), not the good news of the Church, and the result has inevitably been a truncated, cut-down blessing.

Well, what is the Kingdom of God? Of course most clergymen and their followers will define the Kingdom of God very narrowly in terms of their own ideas of the Church, practically at any rate if not theoretically. In other words even when clergymen do not assert that the Kingdom of God and the Church are coterminous, they usually behave practically as if they were and teach a version of the gospel in which this identification is implicit. And of course many clergymen and theologians have explicitly made this identification. But this is not the Christian gospel taught by the Lord Jesus Christ and his apostles, nor by the New Testament. It is not the message of the Bible. Do not misunderstand what I am saying here. I am not claiming that there is no place for assemblies of Christians for the purpose of prayer, teaching, praising God,

[15] V. H. Stanton, *The Jewish and Christian Messiah: A Study in the Earliest History of Christianity* (Edinburgh: T. and T. Clark, 1886), pp. 203f., 206; my emphasis.

[16] Archibald Robertson, *Regnum Dei: Eight Lectures on the Kingdom of God in the History of Christian Thought* (London: Methuen and Co., 1901), p. 8.

discussion, fellowship, encouragement and celebrating the Lord's Supper. Nor am I saying that these things are not important. They are important. But they are not to be put first, as the overriding priority, because if they are they will pervert the biblical priority, as the Church has done for so long and continues to do, and this has resulted and will continue to result in the failure of the true mission of the body of Chirst on earth: the discipling of the *nations*. Why? Because this can only be accomplished as the *Kingdom of God* is manifested on earth and God's will is done on earth as it is in heaven, i.e. among the *nations*. And this is precisely what the New Testament says will be the result of the fulfilling of the Great Commission: "And the seventh angel sounded; and there were great voices in heaven, saying, The kingdoms of *this* world are become the kingdoms of our Lord, and of his Christ; and he shall rule for ever and ever" (Rev. 11:15). Not "The kingdoms of this world are become the Church." The mission is to create Christian *nations*, not merely individual believers. The mission is the coming of the *Kingdom of God on earth*, not bigger and better Churches.

But if the Kingdom of God is not the institutional Church, then what is it? The Kingdom of God is a divine political order that stands over and against all the political orders of men. Its origin and the source of its power and authority are not in this world, but it is God's purpose that the Kingdom should be manifested in *this* world, that the lives of men and nations should be transformed into the Kingdom of God *on earth*, which is what we pray for in the Lord's prayer, what the Lord Jesus Christ commissioned us to pursue in the Great Commission, and what we are told in Rev. 11:15 will be the final result of the Great Commission.

The word *kingdom* is a *political* word. A kingdom has a king, it has a population that is subject to the king, it has its own laws and social forms that embody and incarnate the law of the king in the various social relationships. A kingdom is a political arrangement of all parts of society as a distinctive social order at all levels, both individually and corporately. It is the same with the Kingdom of God. And the Bible makes it clear *how* the Kingdom of God is to be governed and ordered, namely by means of the covenant that God has established with his people as their Lord and Saviour. God always relates to man by means of a *covenant*, and it is in the covenant that we find the details of how this Kingdom is to be manifested as a distinctive social order, *how* God's people are to live as the Kingdom of God.

As believers, redeemed by the Lord Jesus Christ through his sacrificial death on our behalf, we are called *out of* the old world of sin and unbelief, i.e. the political orders of men, and *into* a new *political* order, the Kingdom of God. Christians are not people who have been merely called out of the world of sin and unbelief. They have been called out of the world of sin and unbelief *into* something else, namely a new political order, *the Kingdom of God*. As citizens of the Kingdom of God our calling is to live out the prophetic message of the gospel both as individuals and as the new society, and thereby call the world to repentance. This prophetic message to the world is both verbal and practical. The new society in Christ should not only preach the word of God, but incarnate it in the new social order of the Kingdom, and when this happens the new society becomes a prophetic social order that calls the world to repentance and transforms the world by discipling the nations. This is our calling as believers. If we are to obey this calling faithfully we must put the Kingdom first in everything. Nothing takes priority over the Kingdom. Anything that usurps the priority of the Kingdom of God and his righteousness in our lives is an idol and dishonouring to God's name, even if, indeed *especially* if, that idol is the Church, which, as John Owen declared, is the *greatest* idol that *ever* was in the world.

So what should we do about this? Bear witness to this truth to all your family and friends and in the *Church* you attend; and to this end go to your pastor or minister and ask him to explain how the community of believers is to incarnate the Kingdom of God in its life as a social order, how it is to put the Kingdom of God first. Ask him to teach the covenant. Ask him to explain how we are to live according to the covenant and ask him to demonstrate this in his own life and the life of his family. Ask him to teach his Church members how they are to live as members of the Kingdom of God. And if he cannot or will not do these things, get rid of him, because he is a false prophet, a hireling, who will lead your Church, and probably has already led your Church, into compromise with the world and the inevitable defeat that this leads to.

Here are some practical issues that you can ask him to start explaining. First, how are the members of the Kingdom of God to organise the education of the young so that it conforms to God's will rather than conforming to the dictates of the religion of secular humanism? Second, how is the Kingdom's justice system to be organised so that it conforms to God's will rather than conforming to the dictates of the religion of secular humanism? Third, how should the Kingdom's welfare system be organised so that it conforms to God's will rather than conforming to the dictates of the religion of secular humanism? Fourth, how is the Kingdom's healing ministry and medical system to be organised so that it conforms to God's will rather than conforming to the dictates of the religion of secular humanism? The Bible gives directions for all these things, and it does not call us to be compromised with the world but rather to *transform* the world, to disciple the *nations* to Christ.

This is not the whole of it of course, but it is a start, and these are the things that Jesus prioritised and that the Bible prioritises. We are commanded to teach the good news of the Kingdom of God to all nations. We are commanded to pursue justice (God's righteousness). And the apostle Paul rebuked the Corinthian Christians for not establishing competent courts to deal with disputes between believers. We are told to care for our neighbours. And we are told to heal the sick. All these things receive a higher priority in the teachings of Jesus and the Bible than getting the Sunday morning Church services and rituals correct, and therefore they constitute the true *worship* that God requires of us. In fact the Bible does not prioritise the Sunday Church worship services at all, nor does it define worship as engaging in such services, and our prioritising of these things will achieve nothing in terms of the Great Commission. This prioritising of ritual services is contradicted by the plain teaching of Scripture (cf. James 1:27). It is because the Church has put herself before the Kingdom of God that she is defeated before the world and compromised with it. Such compromise is caused by the idolatry involved in not prioritising what Jesus prioritised, which is the Kingdom of God and his righteousness. And the problem will not be resolved until the Church repents of this idolatry and does the works that God has called her to do instead of the works she wishes to do,—until she prioritises what the Lord has told her to prioritise and abandons her idolatry.

The Lord Jesus Christ came the first time as *Saviour* of the world to establish his *Kingdom* on earth. He will come again when the kingdoms of this world have become *his* Kingdom, but he will come then as *Judge* of the world (2 Tim. 4:1; 1 Pet. 4:5).

"Walk ye not in the statutes of your fathers, neither observe their judgements, neither defile yourselves with their idols: I am the Lord your God; walk in my statutes, and keep my judgements, and do them" (Ezek. 20:18–19).

§4
The Kingdom of God is a Social Order
—*The true social order*

Over the past century Christianity has increasingly ceased to function as public truth in the Western nations. Whatever a society considers to be public truth will inevitably function as the religion of that society. What functions as public truth in modern Western nations is secular humanism. Secular humanism is the religion of the West today. Christianity has been reduced to the status of a mere mystery cult, i.e. a personal salvation cult. But secular humanism is too relativistic to function as a stable foundation for civilisation and must eventually give way to some other religious foundation. Only Christianity can provide a true, stable and lasting foundation for civilisation, and the abandonment of Christianity as public truth in the twentieth century has led to world into chaos. The answer to the chaos that the modern world faces is therefore the renaissance, the rebirth, of Christianity as public truth, i.e. as the religious foundation of our civilisation, in terms of which both individual men and nations, with their civil governments, must organise their whole life by conforming to the precepts and teachings of the Bible. In other words Christianity must be the established religion of all nations. This is precisely what the Great Commission commands us to pursue.

But this will not be possible without the manifestation of the Kingdom of God in the lives of both individual Christians and the Christian communities of all nations as a concrete social order that models to the world what true society should be, and by doing this calls the world to repentance and faith in the Lord Jesus Christ. Without the manifestation on earth in tangible form of this prophetic social order the world will not be won for Christ. The Christian community is to be a light to the world. Only as that light is seen, i.e. only as Christians are seen living as a real social order that transforms the whole life of man, will the world be drawn to it:

"And it shall come to pass in the last days, that the mountain of the Lord's house shall be established in the top of the mountains, and shall be exalted above the hills; and all nations shall flow unto it. And many people shall go and say, Come ye, and let us go up to the mountain of the Lord, to the house of the God of Jacob; and he will teach us his ways, and we will walk in his paths: for out of Zion shall go forth the law, and the word of the Lord from Jerusalem. And he shall judge among the nations, and shall rebuke many peoples: and they shall beat their swords into plowshares, and their spears into pruninghooks: nation shall not lift up swords against nation, neither shall they learn war any more" (Is. 2:2–4).

Although the term *Kingdom of God* is used by Christians it is almost never defined. This is because the worldview of most Christians is dualistic, and the spirituality that dominates their understanding of the faith is a kind of Christianised Gnosticism (see Part One §5 "Gnosticism or the Kingdom of God"). This is what pietism is. But in the pietistic/dualistic worldview it becomes impossible to realise the Kingdom of God in tangible form, and this is why when Christians talk about the Kingdom of God they cannot explain what it is. Ask a Christian what the Kingdom of God is. Ten to one you won't get a proper answer, just a lot of pious waffle about Kingdom values and Kingdom principles at best, and more than likely a load of super-spiritual nonsense that is no more than thinly disguised dualism. The Kingdom of God is incompatible with the dualistic/pietistic worldview, and since that worldview dominates the life of the Church, this is why the Church cannot define the Kingdom of God or actually realise it in any realistic or coherent way. The best the Church does is merely to realise aspects of it. But the Church never gets beyond this. Of course one of the main problems as to why this is the case is the dominance, indeed the very existence, of the clergy, but I will go into that later (see Part One §8, "Smash the Guilds").

So what is the Kingdom of God?

The Kingdom of God is a *counter revolutionary prophetic social order structured by the covenant of grace*—the true society that God intends for mankind. This social order is what all Christians are commanded to seek now, on earth, first, before all else. It is not something that we merely look forward to in the Resurrection, but something we are to seek to make a reality on earth now. Without this being the central goal of our life the assembly of Christians becomes merely a Christian mystery cult—which alas is what has happened today. Therefore, the most important thing we are to seek as Christians in this life is the establishing of this social order as a real community, a real society. Nothing else in our life comes before this according to Jesus, since he tells us to seek first the Kingdom of God and his righteousness. Righteousness means *justice*, not piety. But please note that the assemblies of Christians are only part of this Kingdom, not the whole of it, and it is the usurpation of the Kingdom by the clergy, who are predominantly dualistic cult builders, that has caused and continues to cause such problems for the building of the Kingdom and has reduced the

Kingdom to the Church, over which the clergy exercise control. In other words the Kingdom is reduced to a Christian mystery cult, with the result that it becomes ineffective as the real agent for the transformation of the world, which is what it should be.

§5
GNOSTICISM OR THE KINGDOM OF GOD?

Gnosticism will continue in various ways to undermine the Christian faith until the anthropology underpinning it and driving it is challenged and eradicated. Many Christians who want to challenge Gnosticism will not let go of the animistic anthropology driving it and so their efforts to deal with it will come to nothing and will not change anything. Deal with this animistic anthropology and Gnosticism will be starved of what gives it life. It is pointless railing against Gnosticism unless one is willing to let go of the Graeco-Roman conception of the soul on which it is based. This is what lies at the heart of it. So far the Church in all branches has shown herself unwilling to abandon this false doctrine. The spectre of animism still hangs over the Church's anthropology, and this is ultimately fatal to the further progress of the Great Commission. I believe that dealing with this issue is essential before further progress can be made.

Animism is belief in the existence of the soul. By the word *soul* here I mean the concept of the soul in the pagan and Graeco-Roman sense, not the soul in the biblical sense of *nephesh*, i.e. the *breath of life*. Catharism is probably the best known and most widely recognised of the many Gnostic heresies that were based on this belief and on the basic idea of salvation being the soul's escape from physical matter—which was believed to be the creation of the demiurge or Satan, not God—and its return to the divine essence of which it is believed to be a spark. This dualistic belief system emerged early in Church history and in many different forms and manifestations from the early Gnostic sects to the Messelians, Paulitians, Bogomils and Cathars *et al.* But besides being manifested in these heresies, which were condemned as heresies by the Church, this dualistic perspective also manifested itself within the orthodox Churches as a basic view of reality. The form/matter or spirit/matter dualism of Plato and Graeco-Roman paganism was transformed into the grace/nature dualism of the mediaeval Roman Church, which has continued in the Church into the modern age, even in the Protestant Churches, including the Reformed Churches. This dualism is not just a belief about salvation, though it is that of course, but also an understanding of the nature or structure of reality itself. Anders Nygren called it the Alexandrian worldview.[17] This is antithetical to the biblical view of reality, which has a completely different foundation, namely Creation/Fall/Redemption. This is not to say that Christians influenced by this dualistic principle do not believe in Creation, Fall, and Redemption as biblical doctrines, but rather that these are not seen as the *foundation* of their understanding of *reality*, their *theory of everything*. Their Christianity therefore is conflated with this pagan dualistic idea and as a consequence syncretistic. While this dualism continues to inform their theology and their understanding of the nature and purpose of redemption what they perceive as the upper storey of reality, the spiritual world, will always been seen in antithesis to what they perceive as the lower storey of reality, the world of physical matter, and so their understanding of spirituality will be affected by this. This is about their understanding of the nature of reality, but of course it does also impact their doctrine of redemption.

Catharism flourished in the south-west of what is now France (Languedoc) in the twelfth and thirteenth centuries, but the beliefs of this heretical sect go back way before this. Sometimes the Cathars are called Albigensians. The Cathars got their dualistic beliefs from the Bogomils. Our term *bugger* comes from this heretical sect because the Bogomils were Bulgarian. *Bugger*, which is a corruption of the term Bulgar, meant originally therefore a heretic, i.e. a follower of the Bulgarian heresy (Bogomilism), but it got as-

[17] Andres Nygren, *Agape and Eros* (London: SPCK, 1957, *trans.* Philip S. Watson).

sociated with sodomy because the Cathars, who were followers of the Bulgarian heresy, were accused of being sodomites. As far as I can see there is no evidence for this, but because they theoretically believed and taught that sex is wrong—because it leads to sparks of divinity being trapped in physical bodies—their opponents thought they must be engaging in unnatural sex, and so they were accused of sodomy ("You believe that sex in sinful because it leads to child birth? Well then, you must be a sodomite"—not very smart reasoning to say the least). This accusation often occurs in such situations and it is sometimes difficult to tell if it is true. In the case of the Cathars, however, from what I have read, there seems to be no real evidence for this. The fact is that despite their theoretical rejection of sex they did engage in sex. But extramarital sex was seen as less problematic. It was *marital* sex that they hated the most, because in their understanding it was this that would most likely lead to childbirth—they had various devices of contraception that they used, some magical and useless, others perhaps a bit more likely to have some effect. This is one of the reasons why Catharism was really one of the worst heresies. The practical effects of this heresy were anything but removed from the world of every day life. Catharism demonised marriage or at least marital sex but saw promiscuous extramarital sex as less problematic despite the theoretical condemnation of sex. Of course Catharism is one particular manifestation of the Gnostic worldview. In saying that Gnosticism continues in some form I am not saying that all those influenced by it accept all that the Cathars taught or all that the various other Gnostic sects taught. It is the basic dualistic view of reality and of the soul that is the problem, which can manifest itself in various different ways.

From the biblical perspective human beings do not have souls, i.e. they are not made of two irreconcilable bits, spirit and matter. This is the pagan view. Scripture tells us that when Jacob went down to Egypt seventy souls (*nephesh*) went down with him (Gen 46:26–27). Does this mean that they went down as disembodied spirits and that their bodies remained in Canaan? Of course not! It means seventy *human beings* went down to Egypt. This is not the pagan Graeco-Roman notion of the soul. The biblical notion of the soul is not the same as the Graeco-Roman idea of the soul. Human beings *are* souls. God breathed into Adam the breath of life and he, i.e. the physical creation, *became* a living soul. I do not *have* a soul, I *am* a soul. When we die the breath of life (*nephesh*) leaves us and we cease to be living souls. What makes us human is not the possession of souls, since the animals also have the breath of life (*nephesh*, cf. Eccl. 3:21), but rather our creation in the image of God. Until Christians get rid of this last vestige of animism from their anthropology they will fail to eradicate the spirit of Gnosticism, the Alexandrian worldview, from their lives, and this pagan religious perspective will continue to hamstring their efforts to disciple the nations because the basic idea underpinning this view of salvation is escape from the world, not transformation of the world into the Kingdom of God. The Bible does not teach a doctrine of spiritual deliverance from matter. It teaches deliverance from *sin*, which is the transgression of God's law, and the resurrection of the *body*. Until that resurrection of the body our job is to disciple the nations and therefore transform the world. The Kingdom of God must grow until it displaces and replaces the secular and idolatrous social orders that dominate the nations. The Lord Jesus Christ will not return until the kingdoms of this world have become the Kingdom of our Lord and of his Christ. The dualistic perspective works against this biblical agenda by replacing the Great Commission and the seeking of the Kingdom of God on earth with an escapist agenda based on this false dualistic view of reality and salvation.

§6
The New Christian Dark Age
Just what the world didn't need!

Today Christianity is on the very periphery of learning in our culture. More problematically though, learning is on the very periphery of Christianity. The idea that the Holy Spirit works through the *renewing* of the *mind*, which is what the Bible teaches, has been replaced by the idea that the Holy Spirit works through the *removal* of the *mind*. The dedication of one's mind to God in the service of his Kingdom is looked upon today with suspicion in particular by evangelicals, for whom on the whole anti-intellectualism has become almost an article of faith. This has been going on for a long time but it is getting much worse. When I was a young Christian in my early twenties I was regularly encouraged to burn my books by my more spiritual Charismatic friends, who insisted that my interest in reading was hindering the work of the Holy Spirit in my life. But at least people read the Bible and took it seriously, even if they often misinterpreted its teaching and insisted that all they needed was themselves, the Bible—which they read only in translation and seemed oblivious to the throng of translators surrounding them—and the leading of the Holy Spirit.

Today, forty years on, the Bible has almost been dispensed with altogether. People claim they are Bible believers of course, but it means very little in practice, except perhaps in some Reformed Churches, where things are a little different and Scripture is still given lip service. Otherwise people increasingly rely merely on what they call "pictures" for guidance, i.e. personal revelations in the form of a vision or "picture," not what the Bible teaches. These pictures pop into people's minds. They may say things such as "I had a picture. I don't know what it means but I think it's for you." In house groups people will ask "Has God spoken to you this week, have you had a picture?" The important thing about these "pictures" is that they must be rationally exogenous, since it is believed that the Holy Sprit does not use our minds but rather bypasses the mind. If the Bible is consulted it is used as a source of proof texts for the "pictures," a sort of Bible bingo, where texts are taken out of context, and the purpose is not to understand the message of the Scriptures quoted but to justify and back up the "pictures," which have primary importance. Though, to be honest, even this pretence of a commitment to Scripture is no longer common. The use of the mind in this perspective is unspiritual and necessarily something that is incompatible with being led by the Holy Spirit. It is like being in a preliterate society sometimes. I have heard Christians insist that the mind, the understanding, is a serious hindrance to the work of the Holy Spirit in our lives and it is believed that the Holy Spirit cannot work with people who use their minds. This, to my knowledge, has not happened before in the history of Christianity *except* among *heretical* sects and *cults*.[18] It is a complete rejection both of what the Bible teaches, because we are commanded to worship, i.e. *serve*, God with our whole being, including our *minds* (Mt. 22:37), and a rejection of the historical faith that portends serious problems for the Christian community and the Great Commission. It seems like the Churches, in particular evangelicals, are determined to enter their own bespoke dark age in which the faith becomes a socially irrelevant mystery cult.

What we need is a new commitment to learning and understanding that is at the heart of the Christian faith, and a committed embodiment of that understanding in how we live as a real community that models to the world what the true social order is—the Kingdom of God. Of course, this must be pursued in the Spirit, i.e. by seeking the help, guidance and empowering of the Holy Spirit in the whole person in the whole of life. But the deliberate cutting off of such an important aspect of human life as the function, use and relevance of the mind for the practice of the Christian faith can only be of the very greatest harm not only to the individual believer, but also to the Christian community, the world, and the Kingdom of God, which is meant to grow and increasingly displace, and eventually replace, the godless culture

[18] Among Protestant heretical cults this kind of use of Scripture goes back at least to the pietistic sect established by Count Nikolaus von Zinzendorf in the early eighteenth century. According to Arthur J. Freeman "Zinzendorf also encouraged the devotional use of Scripture. In 1731 he began the use of Daily Texts which persons were to live with for each day, thus enabling them to use Scripture without worrying about how to understand a passage in its context" (www.zinzendorf.com/pages/index.php?id=zinzendorfs-theology). Apparently, Zinzendorf also had a row of headless human figures in his Church to demonstrate the idea that the mysteries of the Christian faith could only be understood by the heart and not by the intellect. On this and the perverse sexual nature of the cult see further R. J. Rushdoony, *Revolt Against Maturity* (Vallecito, CA: Ross House Books, [1977] 1987), p. 46ff.

that surrounds us. We shall either reverse this disastrous trend or the Christian community will enter a new dark age of ignorance in which the blind will stumble from one ditch to another in a pointless wandering of defeat in the wilderness until God raises up a new generation that will serve him by being willing to be led and empowered through the renewing of their *minds* by the Holy Spirit. "Brethren, be not children in understanding: howbeit in malice be ye children, but *in understanding be men*" (1 Cor. 14:20).

§7
WHY PIETISM LEADS TO WORLDLINESS

I have been a Christian for almost fifty years. In all that time I have found very little in most of the Churches I have been in, including the Reformed ones, that is particularly Christian in terms of what I read in the Bible about what Christianity is, other than a weekly gospel sermon that says believing in Jesus is the only way to be saved, salvation in this case being mainly escape from *hell* rather than deliverance from *sin*, and where it is understood as deliverance from sin, the sin has usually been rather narrowly defined in terms of a lack of personal piety not in terms of God's law. The values that dominate the Church today are the same worldly values that dominate our culture, not the values of the Kingdom of God. Although the *terms* are used by Christians in a vague and undefined sense, the concrete realities of the *Kingdom of God* and *God's righteousness*, which Jesus told us to put first, are little discussed in Church, since the Church and its ministry, services, rituals and obedience to man-made rules have taken the place of the Kingdom God and his righteousness (i.e. justice) as the centre of the Christian life.

This problem of worldly values dominating the life of the Church is not confined to the liberal denominations and Churches, which of course make little pretence of conforming to biblical ethics any more. It is no surprise that the value system of the world dominates in these Churches—do they even claim to be Christian in any meaningful sense? But the problem exists no less in the evangelical, Reformed and Charismatic Churches, though there is more pretence in these Churches that this is not the case (well, lets call it what the Bible calls it—hypocrisy). Why?

When the Kingdom is discussed in these Churches it is almost invariably spiritualised into something that has no practical relevance and therefore no meaning or value for real life. If you ask most Christians, including pastors and ministers, what the Kingdom of God is they have no idea how to answer the question other than by falling back onto a dualistic conception of reality that puts the Kingdom and the Christian faith into the upper storey where it has no real bearing on the world that we live in on a daily basis. In other words the answer you get is usually based on some form of Gnostic spirituality, which is the complete antithesis of the Christian religion—and if you find the use of the word *religion* as a means of describing the Christian faith problematic or unacceptable that also is probably because you are working from a dualistic perspective that is contrary to the Christianity of the Bible. Similarly, the word *righteousness* is wrongly understood to mean *piety*, which fits with well with this dualistic perspective, when what it really means is *justice*, which does not fit with the pietistic perspective so well at all. Of course historically the Church has always condemned Gnosticism as a heresy, which of course it is—one of the worst—but even as the Church herself has embraced it with gusto, though often unwittingly.

But you may ask, how is it that the values of our godless society dominate Church life if the prevailing spirituality is dualistic, since Gnostic dualism is hardly the religion of modern secularism? Because this dualism removes most of what it means to be Christian from the realm of daily life and relocates it to the spiritual realm. But everyone has to live in the real world, even pietistic dualists. And so, without a Christian perspective to guide their thoughts and lives in the real day to day world, since the faith is not seen as being relevant to it, Christians unwittingly imbibe the values of the world around them as a means of dealing with everyday life. These values may be given a Christian veneer to dress them up to look Christian, but they are still the values of the world. Dressing up a sow in a pretty frock with pearls and lipstick will not mean that she will behave with decorum and civility at the vicar's tea party. And so the Church becomes corrupted by the values of the world and the Kingdom of God, which Jesus told us to make the central goal of our lives, gets relocated to a spiritual realm that is useless for real life. Once the values of the Kingdom have been exiled to the spiritual realm the values of the world are then all that are left to guide Christians in their daily lives.

So how do we deal with this problem? We have to stop making an idol out of the Church and its forms of service, government, rituals, liturgies, music, and all the other man-made rules that have come to dominate the life of the Church and refocus on the Kingdom of God and his righteousness as our priority. What is the Kingdom? It is a counter-revolutionary prophetic social order founded upon and governed by the covenant of grace that is meant to be manifested and realised on earth among men in this present age and that by its very existence calls men and nations to repentance and obedience to the Lord Jesus Christ. It is not confined to the age to come, nor is it confined to the spiritual realm. All authority in heaven and on earth have been given to the Lord Jesus Christ, the Bible tells us. The Kingdom of God is for this age, now. It is meant to grow until it displaces and replaces the godless secular social orders of the world, and this is meant to continue until all *nations* have embraced it. This is, after all, what the Great Commission teaches. We also have to divest ourselves of the dualistic conception of reality and of the faith that dominates the understanding of most Christians since it is the source of so much error in the Church, both in terms of theology and practice. This world is God's world, and the Lord Jesus Christ came to redeem the whole world, not merely to snatch brands from the fire. Our calling is to bring all things into obedience to the Lord Jesus Christ. As Abraham Kuyper famously said: "there is not a square inch in the whole domain of our human existence over which Christ, who is Sovereign over all, does not cry: 'Mine!'"

§8
Smash the Guilds!

Guild: "an association of artisans or merchants who oversee the practice of their craft/trade in a particular area. The earliest types of guild formed as confraternities of tradesmen. They were organized in a manner something between a professional association, a trade union, a cartel, and a secret society" (Wikipedia). *The Oxford English Dictionary* adds "often having considerable power."

The rules for apostleship as set out by Peter in the first chapter of The Acts of the Apostles are that they must have been with the other apostles and Jesus from the beginning. Notice that they were told to go back to Jerusalem and wait, not go back to Jerusalem and set up the first school of ecclesiastical law-making. In the first chapter of Acts there is no mention of Peter or anyone else being instructed by the Holy Spirit to select a new apostle.

Here is Paul's qualification for apostleship: "Paul, an apostle, not of men, neither by man, but by Jesus Christ, and God the Father, who raised him from the dead" (Gal. 1:1). And here is Paul's rejection of Peter's rule for apostleship, and it is a strongly implied rebuke of the man-made rule: "Wherefore henceforth know we no man after the flesh: yea, though we have known Christ after the flesh, yet now henceforth know we him no more" (2 Cor. 5:16).

Peter's qualification for apostleship was man-made and it is here rejected by Scripture. God thumbed his nose at Peter's rule very quickly by choosing Paul as an apostle, who did not fit any of the criteria Peter insisted on. But the fact that Paul's calling did not conform to the man-made rules set out by Peter dogged him throughout his ministry, as his frequent resort to defending his apostleship among those who questioned it shows, for example among the Galatians, who had been warned off him by the Judaisers, and also among the Corinthians. There seems to have been some kind of whispering or backbiting campaign going on with regard to Paul's apostleship emanating from Jerusalem.

Clearly there is a strong tendency for mankind to form guilds, regardless of what they are actually called. Guilds were a means of controlling a trade or form of livelihood by restricting access to work in a particular field to guild members and demanding conformity to the rules of the guild. By their very nature they are self-serving, abusive and exist to oppress anyone who does not belong to the guild but who works in the same field as the guild members. They exist to suppress individual freedom and as a result they impede economic progress and social amelioration.

The clergy is one of the last remaining mediaeval guilds in Western society, and it is a serious cancer on the body of Christ. It is negative and destructive, and if you doubt this what more proof could you possibly need than the state of the Church today, which in the main is controlled by clergy guilds, which restrict access to ministry to guild members and therefore impede the work of the Kingdom, since God does not accept this guild membership game and does not play by its rules, and, moreover, never has. It is a game of ecclesial power politics invented by men for the benefit of men and has nothing whatsoever to do with God's criteria for ministry, which is *calling*. If you doubt this read the prophets. When you read prophetic books in the Bible what is the first thing that the prophets usually say? Not always but usually? That they were ordained by such and such presbytery or bishop? That they are genuine guild members? No! They say something like "this was not my idea. I was minding my own business when God called me." In other words the first thing they usually say is to explain their *calling*. Indeed the word *prophet* means *one who is called*. The definition of a false prophet is someone who has no calling from God,—but they are well called by men. That is to say, their calling is from men not God. The court prophets were those who were in favour with the establishment, the politicians and priests. They were members of the guild. The prophets called by God did not fit this pattern. They were outsiders. They were not guild members.

Of course the *people* did not want to hear from the prophets God had called either. They also preferred the false prophets, those who were vetted and accepted by the authorities, the court prophets, who would tell them what they wanted to hear. And so it is today on the whole. People prefer the carefully vetted clergymen who will conform to their expectations by justifying their apathy and not rocking the boat, who will keep the status quo. But the Bible gives us a stark warning about this situation: "the prophets prophesy falsely, and the priests rule at their direction; my people love to have it so, but what will you do when the end comes?" (Jer. 5:31).

One of the interesting things about guilds historically is that the Industrial Revolution probably would not have happened if the guilds had been as strong at that time as they were in mediaeval times. It was Cromwell that smashed the power of the guilds in England. He would not tolerate that men who had been in the army fighting tyranny would have to leave the army to find their opportunities to work and earn a living restricted because they were not members of guilds. They were allowed to work regardless of guild membership and rules and the power of the guilds was broken.

It is time to smash the power of the clerical guilds. The growth of the Kingdom of God requires it. The clerical guilds are like a cork in a bottle. They stop anything from going in or coming out of it, as Jesus said of the scribes and Pharisees: "But woe to you, scribes and Pharisees, hypocrites! For you shut up the kingdom of heaven against men; for you neither go in *yourselves,* nor do you allow those who are entering to go in" (Mt. 23:13). The clerical guilds suppress the real ministries needed to facilitate the equipment of the body of Christ for the work of the Kingdom, and therefore the growth of the Kingdom, which is a counter-revolutionary prophetic social order that exists by God's grace to convert and disciple the nations, not a clerical guild that exists to facilitate the growth of self-serving guild support associations, i.e. Church planting. We must seek first the Kingdom of God. *Smash the guilds!*

§9
SACRAMENTS AND MAGIC

There are no sacraments in the Bible. Sacrament is a concept foreign to the biblical worldview. It is interesting to observe that where sacramental thinking is strong, covenantal thinking is usually very weak, often non-existent. What are usually misconstrued as sacraments in Scripture are really covenant signs, not sacraments.

A *sacramentum* was originally a sum of money deposited with a representative of the State (one of the *tresviri capitales*) when a Roman citizen went to court. The party that lost his case lost his *sacramentum*, which was then used to defray the costs of the public works, temples and sacrifices. It was called a *sacramentum* either because if forfeited it was used for religious purposes or, more probably, because it was deposited in a sacred place.[19] It later came to mean an *oath*, such as that sworn by the legionaries, but it was not restricted to legionary oaths. It subsequently came to mean a *mystery*, and then the Church decided it would henceforth mean something it had never meant before, namely the *outward sign of an inward grace*. Sacrament, in the sense that the word is used today and by the Church throughout most of history, was an invention of the Church to bolster up the growing ritualisation of the faith and concentration of power in the hands of a priesthood, and its development went, and still goes, hand in hand with the abandonment of covenant. The concept is alien to biblical theology. Where sacramental theology is strong covenantal theology is usually very weak. The degree to which one accepts the whole idea of sacraments is the degree to which one fails to understand biblical covenantal theology and adopts a magical instead of a covenantal understanding of the Christian faith. It is also the degree to which Christianity is abandoned as a religion and becomes a mere mystery cult instead. Circumcision, the Passover, Baptism and the Lord's Supper (i.e. the *agape*, the Christian Passover) are

[19] C. T. Lewis and C. Short, *A Latin Dictionary* (Oxford: The Clarendon Press, [1879] 1927), p. 1611*c*.

covenant rites,—signs and seals of the covenant—not sacraments. The concept of sacrament in the sense used by the Church is an idea foreign to Scripture. There are no sacraments in the Bible. The word was not even used in the sense in which it is used today and has been used throughout most of Church history until around the third century A.D. (it was first used in this sense by Tertullian, *c.* 155–240 A.D.).

Fundamental to the concept of sacrament is the idea that the correct performance of ritual can produce an effect in the recipient and indeed even in the external world, so that all one needs to do to practice the faith and even reform the world is to practice the correct liturgy in the Church, and where the liturgy is deemed to be defective, to reform the liturgy according to whichever sacramental theory one believes to be correct. The correct term for this kind of belief is *magic*. The performance of what is deemed to be correct ritual underpins all forms of magic. Belief in the power of ritual (magic) is thoroughly pagan, and yet it is this belief that structures, governs and manifests itself in the vast majority of Christian Churches today, as indeed it has done throughout the greater part of the history of the Church, and this is so for Protestant and Charismatic Churches no less than traditional Episcopal Churches.

The Bible has very little to say about ritual in the *ecclesia*, the Christian assembly, and Jesus himself seems to have spoken and behaved in such a way that it is impossible to derive any form of ritual from his teaching or actions. In fact, the rituals of the Church in the main derive not from the Bible (although justification for ritual itself is often incorrectly derived from a mistaken understanding of the Old Testament temple sacrifices), but rather from pagan Roman religious rituals, which were stripped of their pagan content and then given a superficial Christian veneer. Belief in the power of ritual, i.e. magic, replaced the covenant. But Christianity does not work by magic. God works through the lives of his people, through their obedience to his word (the covenant of grace), in living as the true society, the Kingdom of God, which is a counter-revolutionary prophetic social order, the purpose of which is to glorify God by converting all the nations, thereby transforming the world, so that when the Lord Jesus returns the kingdoms of this world will have become the Kingdom of our Lord and of his Christ (Rev. 11:15). This is about as far from what goes on in most Churches today as it is possible to get.

The Christian community today desperately faces the need for a renaissance as great as, indeed even greater than, the Reformation of the sixteenth century. But it is unlikely that such a renaissance will ever take place while the present structures of Church authority and the official magic that supports them retain their stranglehold on the body of Christ. It seems therefore inevitable that the precursor to such a renaissance can only be a complete collapse and final discarding of those structures and the ideologies that give them meaning and life. If the house is to be rebuilt again according to the Lord's design, the crooked foundations on which it previously stood for so long must be cleared away for good.

§10
TO WHAT SHALL WE COMPARE THESE TIMES?

Someone on a discussion group I am on recently asked this question: "Are there any parallels between our current time and the pre-Reformation period?" My answer was yes, there are, but more importantly, what we need to understand more than these parallels with pre-Reformation times are the parallels between now and pre-Constantinian imperial Rome. We face a situation today that has not existed since before Constantine, since the time of the pagan Roman emperors. This was not the case in pre-Reformation times. It is these parallels with pagan Rome that we need to understand today. There is an aphorism that says "Nature abhors a vacuum."[20] The unpalatable truth is that the vacuum left by the Christian community's abandonment of its calling to be salt and light to the

[20] This statement has been attributed to Aristotle and was later restated by others such as Galileo. It was originally meant in a physical sense rather than as a social metaphor.

nations is being filled increasingly by the values of a worldview that is in many respects similar to that of pagan imperial Rome, and it is this worldview that is shaping our modern world.

Since the time of Constantine until fairly recently Western society has acknowledged the higher law of God and believed that all human government and law must recognise and conform to the higher law of God. This was never perfectly practised of course, and there was much failure in this respect and many tyrants who wanted it otherwise. But the principle was acknowledged and understood. It was impossible in mediaeval times to swear away one's higher allegiance to God. In every oath of fealty that was taken there was always a saving for the faith due to God, i.e. one swore allegiance to one's lord in life and limb, to obey in all things, save only in one's duty to God. No man could swear away his higher duty to God and no prince could legitimately demand this of him. "In the *Leges Henrici* we may find the high-water-mark of English vassalism. Every man owed faith to his lord of life and limb and earthly worship, and must observe his lord's command in all that is honourable and proper, saving the faith due to God and the ruler of his land; but theft, treason, murder, or anything that is against God and the catholic faith, such things are to be commanded by none, and done by none. Saving these, however, faith must be kept to lords, more especially to a liege lord, and without his consent one may have no other lord."[21]

No matter how bad things got, and they did get pretty bad, man's higher duty to God was always acknowledged. It is this fact that gives meaning to the Christian doctrine of the rule of law, which did not mean that all a prince had to do to get his own way was to pass a law permitting him to do whatever he liked, but rather that all law of princes or States must conform to the higher law of God. "A human law could not be valid in contradiction to divine law. In the *Doctor and Student* these two propositions are clearly stated. 'When the law eternal or the will of God is known to His creatures reasonable by the light of natural understanding, or by

[21] F. Pollock and F. W. Maitland, *The History of English Law Before the Time of Edward I* (Cambridge University Press, 1911), Vol. I, p. 300.

the light of natural reason, that is called the law of reason: and when it is showed of heavenly revelation . . . then it is called the law of God. And when it is showed unto him by order of a Prince, or of any other secondary governor, that hath power to set law upon his subjects, then it is called the law of man, though originally it be made of God.' 'For if any law made of men bind any person to anything that is against the said laws (the law of reason or the law of God) it is no law but a corruption and a manifest error'"[22] (see the diagram on page 51). Or, as a doctrine of English common law put it, "Any law is or of right ought to be according to the law of God."[23] The prince or State was under God. Even in the worst tyrannies this was understood, even though abused.

This is no longer the case today. Secular humanist States and governments acknowledge no higher law than their own. They are a law unto themselves. And in making themselves the highest law in the land, beyond which there is no appeal to the higher law of God, they effectively put themselves in the place of God,—i.e. they effectively claim the attributes of God. In Western history one has to go back to the time before Constantine, to the pagan Roman emperors, to find this divine status of the prince or State. This is what attribution of divinity to the Roman emperors really meant. It was a political fact—the emperors did not really believe they were divine (except those that were insane), but they did see Roman law as ultimate, and that man's allegiance to Rome came first, before all else, and this was symbolised in the imperial cult, i.e. emperor worship. This was a political issue not a religious issue in the narrow sense, i.e. a question of personal devotion to a deity. Rome did not care whom one worshipped as a personal deity, and there were many mystery cults with different gods that one could participate in. Rome wanted Christians to behave in the same way that members of the mystery cults behaved, i.e. worship

[22] *Doctor and Student: or Dialogues between A Doctor of Divinity and A Student in the Laws of England* was an important and well-known treatise on English law by Christopher Saint Germain published in 1523 in Latin and in 1531 in English.

[23] Both quotations cited in A. K. R. Kiralfy, *Potter's Historical Introduction to English Law* (London: Sweet and Maxwell Ltd, Fourth Edition, 1958), pp. 578f., 33. The latter statement is taken from a Year Book in the reign of Henry VII.

THE CHRISTIAN DOCTRINE OF THE RULE OF LAW
(based on Christopher Saint Germain's, *Doctor and Student*, 1523)

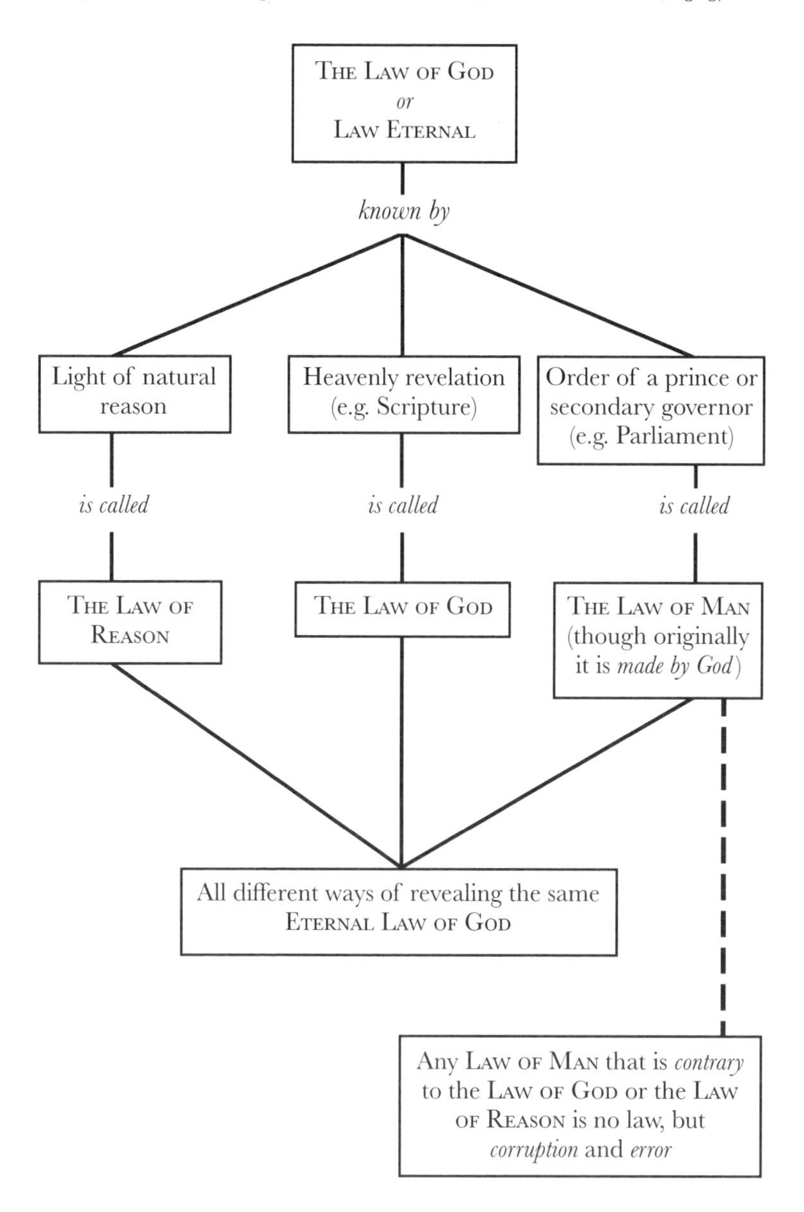

Christ to your hearts' content in your private devotions, but your politics must be the politics of Rome, you must give your political allegiance to Rome. The Christians refused and said no, Jesus is Lord, and claimed to be members of his *ecclesia* first—*ecclesia* is a political term not a cultic term.[24] This was a political statement of rebellion against Rome and treason against Rome. Rome, symbolised by emperor worship, was in the place of God. No higher law or Lord was acknowledged or permitted.

From the time of Constantine onwards this changed. No matter how badly the principle of man's higher duty to God was practised it was still understood. Today though, for the first time since the age of the pagan Roman emperors the denial of this principle is a reality. Modern States and politicians no longer see themselves as bound by God's higher law and no longer acknowledge this principle. Even where there is a theoretical and constitutional commitment to it, as in Britain, in practice it is denied and Parliament no longer takes account of it in its law-making. In this respect there are parallels between our political system and that of ancient pre-Christian imperial Rome.

But it gets worse. This principle is no longer even believed in the Church on the whole. And the reason that this principle is no longer acknowledged by the State is because the Church herself has abandoned it. The apostasy of the Church has paved the way and lighted the path to the apostasy of the State.

Some years ago I spent some time studying and reading up on the history of the mediaeval period, from late classical times onward, and particularly (though not exclusively) the history of heresy, particularly the dualist heresies, from the Manichees through to the Bogomils and onto the Cathars. One of the things that stood out about this, and that I saw being frequently brought up by most of the authors I read is this: the orthodox accept the Old Testament, Moses, and the law of God; the heretics reject them. The

[24] For a more detailed explanation of this see my book *The Politics of God and the Politics of Man: Essays on Politics, Religion and Social Order* (Kuyper Foundation, 2016), Chapter Two (available from the Kuyper Foundation website: www.kuyper.org/books).

heretics have a truncated Scripture. Time and again this comes out. The orthodox accept the law of Moses; the heretics reject it. Of course this does not mean that the orthodox had a perfect understanding or completely consistent theology and practice of the law; far from it (none of us have—we all have a long way to go). But there was a principle that was accepted by the orthodox and rejected by the heretics. While in the past, however imperfectly the orthodox practised the faith (and at times it is truly excruciating to read the history of orthodoxy let alone the history of heresy), the law of God, the Old Testament and Moses have in principle been accepted by the orthodox. Those that rejected these were the heretics.

Today, this situation is reversed. The Church as a whole now rejects the Old Testament, Moses and the law of God; those who accept these are considered to have a faulty and "legalistic" theology at best, even if they are not considered heretical (and often they are). The Church of the twentieth and twenty-first century is heretical to the core because of this. "New Testament Christianity" is heretical at heart. There were no New Testament Christians in the New Testament. The Christians of New Testament times did not have a New Testament. The Scripture of Christians in the New Testament was the Old Testament.

When did the New Testament replace the Old? Not in the apostolic age. Not in the sub-apostolic age. Not in mediaeval times. Not at the time of the Reformation. Not until the twentieth century—except among the heretics. Until the twentieth century, the rejection of the Old Testament, Moses and the law of God was a definitive feature of heresy. It still is. This is the age of heresy.

This continues to be a highly relevant and problematic issue. Throughout the two thousand year history of Christianity there have only been two groups of people that have rejected the Old Testament, Moses and the law of God: heretics and modern evangelicals. Or rather, I should perhaps really say, only one group of people: heretics. The modern apostate and heretical Church has led the world to ruin. It is time for the salt that has lost its saltiness to be thrown out and trampled underfoot, time for new wineskins.

PART TWO

HOW TO DISCIPLE THE NATIONS

SCRIPTURE READINGS

Numbers chapter 13

"And the Lord spake unto Moses, saying, Send thou men, that they may search the land of Canaan, which I give unto the children of Israel: of every tribe of their fathers shall ye send a man, every one a ruler among them. And Moses by the commandment of the Lord sent them from the wilderness of Paran: all those men were heads of the children of Israel. And these were their names: of the tribe of Reuben, Shammua the son of Zaccur. Of the tribe of Simeon, Shaphat the son of Hori. Of the tribe of Judah, Caleb the son of Jephunneh. Of the tribe of Issachar, Igal the son of Joseph. Of the tribe of Ephraim, Oshea the son of Nun. Of the tribe of Benjamin, Palti the son of Raphu. Of the tribe of Zebulun, Gaddiel the son of Sodi. Of the tribe of Joseph, namely, of the tribe of Manasseh, Gaddi the son of Susi. Of the tribe of Dan, Ammiel the son of Gemalli. Of the tribe of Asher, Sethur the son of Michael. Of the tribe of Naphtali, Nahbi the son of Vophsi. Of the tribe of Gad, Geuel the son of Machi. These are the names of the men which Moses sent to spy out the land. And Moses called Oshea the son of Nun Jehoshua. And Moses sent them to spy out the land of Canaan, and said unto them, Get you up this way southward, and go up into the mountain: And see the land, what it is, and the people that dwelleth therein, whether they be strong or weak, few or many; And what the land is that they dwell in, whether it be good or bad; and what cities they be that they dwell in, whether in tents, or in strong holds; And what the land is, whether it be fat or lean, whether there be wood therein, or not. And be ye of good courage, and bring of the fruit of the land. Now the time was the time of the first ripe grapes. So they went up, and searched the land from the wilderness of Zin unto Rehob, as men come to Hamath. And they ascended by the south, and came unto Hebron; where Ahiman, Sheshai, and Talmai, the children of Anak, were. (Now Hebron was built seven years before Zoan in Egypt.) And they came unto the brook of Eshcol, and cut down from thence a branch with one cluster of grapes, and they bare it between two upon a staff; and they brought of the pomegranates, and of the figs. The place was called the brook Eshcol, because of the cluster of grapes which the children of Israel cut down from thence. And they returned from searching of the land after forty days. And they went and came to Moses, and to Aaron, and to all the congregation of the children of Israel, unto the wilderness of Paran, to Kadesh; and brought back word unto them, and unto all the congregation, and shewed them the fruit of the land. And they told him, and said, We came unto the land whither thou sentest us, and surely it floweth with milk and honey; and this is the fruit of it. Nevertheless the people be strong that dwell in the land, and the cities are walled, and very great: and moreover we saw the children of Anak there. The Amalekites dwell in the land of the south: and the Hittites, and the Jebusites, and the Amorites, dwell in the mountains: and the Canaanites dwell by the sea, and by the coast of Jordan. And Caleb stilled the people before Moses, and said, Let us go up at once, and possess it; for we are well able to overcome it. But the men that went up with him said, We be not able to go up against the people; for they are stronger than we. And they brought up an evil report of the land which they had searched unto the children of Israel, saying, The land, through which we have gone to search it, is a land that eateth up the inhabitants thereof; and all the people that we saw in it are men of a great stature. And there we saw the giants, the sons of Anak, which come of the giants: and we were in our own sight as grasshoppers, and so we were in their sight."

ISAIAH 2:2–4

"And it shall come to pass in the last days, that the mountain of the Lord's house shall be established in the top of the mountains, and shall be exalted above the hills; and all nations shall flow unto it. And many people shall go and say, Come ye, and let us go up to the mountain of the Lord, to the house of the God of Jacob; and he will teach us of his ways, and we will walk in his paths: for out of Zion shall go forth the law, and the word of the Lord from Jerusalem. And he shall judge among the nations, and shall rebuke many people: and they shall beat their swords into plowshares, and their spears into pruninghooks: nation shall not lift up sword against nation, neither shall they learn war any more."

MATTHEW 6:33

"But seek ye first the kingdom of God, and his righteousness; and all these things shall be added unto you."

MATHEW 28:18–20

"And Jesus came and spake unto them, saying, All power is given unto me in heaven and in earth. Go ye therefore, and teach all nations, baptizing them in the name of the Father, and of the Son, and of the Holy Ghost: Teaching them to observe all things whatsoever I have commanded you: and, lo, I am with you alway, *even* unto the end of the world."

REV. 11:15

"And the seventh angel sounded; and there were great voices in heaven, saying, The kingdoms of this world are become *the kingdoms* of our Lord, and of his Christ; and he shall reign for ever and ever."

HOW TO DISCIPLE THE NATIONS

§I
The Churches are not places for serious Christians to be

I recently came across the following statement: "The Churches are not places for serious Christians to be." Hard as it may be to accept this, I believe it is for the most part true and that unless we accept and embrace this truth we shall fail to understand the biblical teaching and emphasis, which is not on the *Church*, but rather on the *Kingdom of God*, and furthermore, we shall fail in our calling to pursue the Great Commission, which is not a command to plant Churches, but rather a command to *disciple* the *nations*. This does not mean, however, that there are no serious Christians in the Churches. There are. But they do tend to have a hard time of it. What we call the Church today has travelled a long way from the assemblies of Christians in the New Testament, and on this journey the institution we know today as the Church has not only lost its original meaning and purpose but has been transformed into the greatest foe of the Kingdom of God that exists and, to use the words of John Owen, the greatest idol that ever was in the world.

On the *positive* side of the equation, the Church as a liturgical institution,—i.e. the Church you "go to" on a Sunday morning (please observe my definition[25])—has, throughout the course of Christian history, accomplished almost *nothing*. She converted

[25] I understand that the term *Church* can be defined in much broader terms than this, and indeed if we are to use the term meaningfully it should be understood in much broader terms, but unfortunately this is not usually the case. When the

neither the West nor the East, either in the earliest times of the Christian faith or at any time since. On the *negative* side, this Church has set herself up as the main rival of and in opposition to the Kingdom of God and consequently has been the greatest hindrance to the progress of the Kingdom and one of the main persecutors of the faithful throughout the greater part of Christian history.

I know this sounds controversial and radical, but please bear with me. What I mean will become clear. But we need to start first with the Great Commission.

§2
MISTRANSLATING THE GREAT COMMISSION

The modern English translation of the first part of the Great Commission (Mt. 28:19) is ambiguous. The reason for this is that English, strictly speaking, has no verb meaning *to disciple*. *The Concise Oxford English Dictionary* (Eighth Edition) lists the word *disciple* as a noun only. The nearest verb to it is *to discipline*, which, although not without some relevance for what it means to be a disciple of Christ, does not convey the meaning of the Greek term used (*matheteusate*, aor. act. imp. of *matheteuo*). Modern English translations get round this by using the phrase *make disciples of*. The Greek verb means *to be a disciple*.[26] In the koine Greek of the New Testament, which was the everyday language spoken by the people of the Roman empire in the first century, this verb is used transitively to mean *to disciple*.[27] In Mt. 28.19 it is an imperative with "all the nations" (*panta ta ethne*) as the object of the command. In other words the

---

word is used it is predominantly understood to mean the Church as a liturgical institution with its rituals, discipline and bureaucracy governed by clergymen. Nevertheless, it is a problematic word and a mistranslation of the Greek word *ecclesia*. On the etymology and meaning of the term see §1 "Church (*kyrikon*)" in the Definition of Terms above.

[26] G. Abbott-Smith, *op. cit.*, p. 275.

[27] Gerhard Kittel and Gerhard Friedrich, *op. cit.*, Vol. IV, p. 146; F. Blass and A.

Great Commission does *not* say "go and make disciples of all nations." Rather, it says "go and disciple all the nations," i.e. go and *make all nations my disciples.*

Because there is, strictly speaking, no single term in English that translates this Greek verb the Authorised Version, following Tyndale and the Geneva Bible, translates the first part of the Great Commission as "Go ye therefore, and *teach* all nations." This translation preserves the grammar of the original Greek accurately. Most modern translations, however, have followed the translators of the Revised Version, which reads: "Go ye therefore and *make disciples of* all the nations." The New American Standard Bible reads: "Go therefore and *make disciples of* all the nations." Likewise the Revised Standard Version reads: "Go therefore and *make disciples of* all nations." Even the New King James Version changes the Authorised Version's wording to "Go therefore and *make disciples of* all the nations," failing completely to observe an important reason for keeping the Authorised Version's "*teach* all nations" (see the diagram on p. 63).

There are two problems with this modern translation: first, it turns the Greek verb *to disciple* (*matheteuo*) into the English verb *to make*, and the direct object of this verb becomes the English noun *disciples* instead of *nations*. Second, it turns the object of the Greek verb into a genitive; i.e. it turns the word "nations," which in the Greek is in the accusative case (the case of the direct object), into a genitive case governed by the preposition "of," which is not in the Greek. This gives us an English phrase that is ambiguous in the place of a Greek phrase that is not ambiguous.

The modern English translation could be taken to mean just what the Greek says, i.e. "make the *nations* the disciples of Christ." But it does not have to be understood in this way. It is ambiguous, vague. It could equally be taken to mean something else, and unfortunately in modern times, because of the pietistic theological consensus that has come to dominate the Church's understanding

---

Debrunner, *A Greek Grammar of the New Testament and Other Early Christian Literature* (Cambridge University Press, 1961, trans. Robert W. Funk), §148, p. 82*af*.

of the faith, it has overwhelmingly been taken to mean something else, namely "make disciples *from among* all the nations." This is a perfectly reasonable and correct understanding of the English. But it is an incorrect rendering of the Greek. The Greek says that we are to go and disciple the *nations*, not make disciples *of* the nations, i.e. *from among* the nations.

Many people misunderstand the Great Commission as a command to make disciples of people from all nations. This is not what Jesus commanded his disciples to do in the Great Commission. Rather, he commanded us to disciple the nations *as* nations. i.e. to make Christian *nations*.

The vagueness of the modern English translation has led to, or at least has helped to confirm in the opinion of most Christians today, an incorrect understanding of the Great Commission. This misconception has been so readily accepted because of the pietistic nature of contemporary Christian belief, i.e. the idea that the Christian faith relates to an understanding of spirituality that is narrowly focused on the individual's private devotional life, Church worship—which is increasingly equated with singing choruses—and the "afterlife," all things that relate to the upper storey of reality in the dualistic worldview. In this perspective the faith is not seen as having a direct bearing on the everyday issues that determine so much of our lives—for example education, politics, welfare, the economy, the arts, business, science, medicine and culture generally. The Christian faith is not seen as addressing these areas at all by the vast majority of Christians today. The faith has been privatised and as a result has been neutered of its power to transform society. In this context the misreading of the Great Commission as a command to make individual disciples from among the nations has seemed natural. But the modern context has distorted the Church's understanding of the Bible and the modern understanding of the Great Commission is erroneous.

But how do we disciple the nations? It is impossible to disciple the nations without making individual disciples. But it is possible to make individual disciples *without* going on to disciple the *nations*. The difference is one of *vision* and *mission*. The Great Commission

Matthew 28:19a—Comparison of English Translations with the Greek Original

Greek	πορευθέντες	οὖν	μαθητεύσατε	πάντα τὰ ἔθνη
	nom. pl. masc. part. aor. of πορεύομαι		2nd pers. pl. aor. imper. act. of μαθητεύω	acc. neuter pl. case of direct object
Literal	Going	therefore	disciple	all the nations
Tyndale	Go	therefore	and teach	all nations
Geneva	Go	therefore	and teach	all nations
AV	Go ye	therefore	and teach	all nations
RV	Go ye	therefore	and make disciples of	all the nations
NASB	Go	therefore	and make disciples of	all the nations
RSV	Go	therefore	and make disciples of	all nations
NKJ	Go	therefore	and make disciples of	all the nations
NIV	Therefore go		and make disciples of	all nations
JBP	You, then, are to go		and make disciples of	all the nations

is a command to *disciple* the *nations*. This means that we must make individual disciples, of course, but it does not stop there. It goes further. It means that the *nations* must submit to the Lord Jesus Christ and become *Christian* nations. This is what the Bible teaches and it is what was understood to be the case in previous ages. The idea that the Great Commission is just about making individual disciples, soul saving, is a new idea, in the English speaking world roughly coterminous with the diabolical mistranslation of the Great Commission in the Revised Version of the Bible,[28] which almost all modern English translations have followed.[29]

§3
HOW THE WEST WAS CONVERTED

But how do we disciple the *nations* rather than just making individual disciples from among the nations? This is a reasonable question. One popular answer to this question is this: we must all go and live in the *cities*, at the crossroads of civilisation, where we can have most effect. At first this may seem very plausible. It does not seem like a bad answer, indeed it seems very reasonable. Many think this really is what Christians should do: move into the inner

[28] I am aware of the Radical Reformation origins of this belief and its growing and corrupting influence from the time of the Reformation onwards, particularly in the antipaedobaptist and separatist sects, and also that this influence may have been at work in the process that led to the corruption of the translation of Mt. 28:19 in the Revised Version of the Bible. But it was in the twentieth century that this influence became mainstream, and the mistranslation of this Scripture in the Revised Version is roughly coterminous with the expansion of this erroneous understanding of the Great Commission in the Church as a whole.

[29] An exception to this is the New English Bible, which translates the first part of the Great Commission as "Go forth therefore and make all nations my disciples." Unfortunately this excellent translation of the first part of the Great Commission is completely ruined by the mistranslation of the second half: "baptise *men everywhere* in the name of the Father and the Son and the Holy Spirit, and teach them to observe all that I have commended you" (my italics). The problem is the substitution of "men everywhere" for "them," so that there is no longer a pronoun that refers back to the "nations" and the pronoun "them" in verse 20 is consequently understood as referring back to "men everywhere," which is er-

city *en masse*. But here is the interesting thing about this answer: it is almost exactly the *opposite* of how Europe was actually converted to Christianity.

The unpalatable truth is that it was the *monasteries* and the *monks* that converted Europe to the Christian faith. And they did the opposite of this. They went off into the wilderness, not into the cities. They withdrew. Now I am not advocating that we should necessarily do the same, but I am not advocating that we should all move into the cities either. I think *both* these answers miss the point, and that what made the difference for the monasteries was not that they went into the wilderness, though often once they had gone into the wilderness communities started developing around them, i.e. they attracted others to them.

Nor am I advocating that we set up monasteries. There were serious problems with the monasteries. They did accomplish much and it was not all bad by any means, but there were serious problems that we must not imitate. They were first, *communistic*, and communism is *not* a biblical ideal. In fact communism contradicts the biblical ideal of what a Christian social order should be, e.g. the inviolability of private property, including property in land, the importance of inheritance etc.[30] Second they were *celibate*, at least from the high Middle Ages onwards, and celibacy is not a biblical ideal, in fact it is contrary to the biblical ideal of family life. I am *not* saying of course that it is wrong for someone to be single as such. Celibacy, however, is the *ideology* of singleness, i.e. the idea that celibacy is a *higher spiritual condition*, and therefore *required* of those

---

roneously introduced in verse 19. A command to baptise *men everywhere* constitutes a mission that is very different from a command to baptise all the *nations*, and it is the latter that the Greek text gives us not the former. The focus of the mission is changed completely by the New English Bible's mistranslation. Instead of a command to baptise and teach the law of God to the nations we have an individualistic focus that completely fails to do justice to the socio-political implications of the Great Commission. On the relevance—or rather I should say *irrelevance*—of the gender disagreement between the noun "nations" (*ethne*) and its pronoun "them" (*autous*) see the Excursus in my essay *The Great Decommission* (Taunton: Kuyper Foundation, 2011), p. 36ff.

[30] For more on this see Chapter Six, "Communism in the New Testament" in my book *The Politics of God and the Politics of Man*, pp. 222–244.

with a vocation in Christian community or ministry. This idea flies flat in the face of biblical teaching. Third, they made a new rule for themselves to function as the basis of their social order. There was the rule of St Augustine, the rule St Benedict, the rule of St Francis of Assisi etc. These rules replaced the biblical rule that God has given us in the Bible to function as the basis of a Christian social order, namely, the covenant. Our rule for life is the covenant. The Bible is the rule for life, for the life of the individual and for the life of the society of which he is a member. Fourth, the methods they sometimes used in the conversion of Europe were not biblical and not good; for example, the conversion of the king or tribal leader and then the conversion of the population to the Christian faith by force. This is a complex subject however, and it is not the only way that conversion happened, and even where it may appear to be so there were often other factors at work that need to be considered and that mitigate the idea that the baptism of a whole tribe on the conversion of the tribal leader was necessarily wrong.

All these things created immense problems for the monasteries themselves and for the pursuit of the Kingdom of God and the Great Commission, notwithstanding the good they did, and we must not imitate them in this. But this does not mean that the monasteries and monks did no good, nor does it mean there are not things that we can learn from them. There are.

Most importantly, they believed that Christianity should manifest as an *alternative social order* to the world, a social order that is incompatible with the social orders of men, and that is based on a completely different set of values to the values of the world. This is what they got right in principle, and so powerful was this idea that despite all the problems and compromises, which were many and serious, yet still they *transformed* Europe. Europe was converted by the monasteries and the monks.

Now, I am *not* proposing that we go back to setting up monasteries. But I am saying that we need to take seriously the idea that the Christian faith must manifest as an *alternative social order* to the social orders of the world.

§4
How to disciple the nations

Well you may ask, if we should not go back to the monasteries, *then what*? How do *we* disciple the nations today? By pursuing the *Kingdom of God* and his *righteousness*, not only as individuals, but also as a *community of believers*, as the society of faith in the Lord Jesus Christ. How do we pursue the Kingdom of God and his righteousness? Well, righteousness (*dikaiosyne*), is "conformity to the Divine will in purpose, thought and action."[31] We understand this with regard to the individual well enough. But it is the same with society. Our social order must conform to the divine will in purpose, thought and action.

All kingdoms are social orders. Even the animal kingdoms are social orders. A kingdom necessarily means there is a ruler, an ultimate lord, who issues laws to which those who live in his kingdom must be subject, that there is a society that lives and functions in terms of the will of the king both in terms of individual lives and as a community. A kingdom is not just a haphazard collection of individuals. It is a society. The root meaning of the word *society* is the Latin verb *socio*, which means *to unite, to share, to have in common*. The noun *societas* means an *alliance*, a *partnership*. A kingdom is made up of people who have something in common, who share a particular kind of life together, and that life is one that is determined by the will of the king. In their corporate life together those who constitute a nation demonstrate their understanding and practice of the meaning of life, which they derive from the ultimate authority in that society, which in pagan societies was often the sacral king, half human half divine, and in Christian nations that ultimate authority is God, in terms of whose law even the earthly king or magistrate must submit and rule. Likewise in republics and democracies, the government must be subject to the ultimate authority. But not only the government, the whole cultural life of society is to be a manifestation of the divine will in purpose thought and action.

[31] G. Abbott-Smith, *op. cit.*, p. 116.

Discipleship requires modelling the Christian life to someone as well as teaching doctrine. Discipleship is essentially the same thing as apprenticeship. It is not going to school and learning something in a purely decontextualised intellectual setting, but learning on the job, living the job. The apprentice learns from the one to whom he is apprenticed. Likewise with the disciple. Discipleship is about the practical incarnation of the teaching in the life lived and the disciple learns how to live the Christian life from the one who models for him what it means to live the Christian life. This is obvious with individual discipleship. But how do we disciple a nation? Well, we must model to the world what the *true society*, the *true social order*, should be by the way we live as a *community*.

When I speak of community I do not mean a commune or communist society. When I have spoken about the need for Christian community in the past I have often been misunderstood to mean a commune, and even when I have explained that this is not what I mean people have found it difficult to think of this in any other terms, at least until I brought a critique of communism into this message. Community does not necessitate living in communes or the organisation of society on socialist or communist lines. In fact I would argue that socialism and communism are inimical to real community, at least community in the biblical sense, which is what true community should be. A community is a *society*, a *social order*. The Kingdom of God is the community that we should be seeking. What then is the Kingdom of God?

The Kingdom of God is a counter-revolutionary prophetic *social order* structured by the covenant of grace that has come into this world now and is meant to grow until it displaces and eventually replaces the social orders of men. Its values are not the values of the world. The Kingdom of God is not *of* this world, i.e. its origin, meaning, purpose and authority come from God, not from the kingdoms of this world, but it is meant to be manifested *in this world now* thereby transforming this world, so that on the Last Day it will be said that "The kingdoms of *this* world are becomes the kingdoms of our Lord and of his Christ" (Rev. 11:15). Many Christians think that the Kingdom of God is otherworldly and that righteousness means piety, and this is why they think it requires withdrawal from the world. But in truth seeking the Kingdom of God and God's righteousness means seeking to establish a just social order that conforms to God's will. It is the *opposite* of pietism and withdrawal.

The early Christians at the time of the Roman persecutions were not persecuted for worshipping Jesus. They were persecuted for being *imperium in imperio*, i.e. for constituting themselves as an alternative social order to the social order of Rome, and this the Roman authorities could not tolerate. For the Romans this was *treason*, which is a political offence. They were not persecuted for worshipping Jesus as God, but for not submitting to the Roman political order,—effectively for not worshipping the Roman State as God. And by the way, something very similar to this Roman attitude is what is developing rapidly now in modern Western States, primarily because Christians have ceased to be salt and light to the nations, i.e. they have ceased to model what true social order should be to the world and have sought pietistic withdrawal from the world instead. As a result the modern Church is escapist rather than redemptive.

The Kingdom of God is a *social order*. We must model the Kingdom of God to the world. The Kingdom of God is the true social order that God requires of us. Christians should be in their life together the alternative social order that is the Kingdom of God, which is based on a completely different set of values to the values of the world.

Incidentally, it is interesting to note that where people are part of a strong, loving and supportive community, they get ill much less, and when they do get ill they recover much more quickly. This in itself sheds light on the sad fact that despite Jesus' having told us to preach the gospel and heal the sick, healing in the Churches is hit and miss at best. Often Churches are not communities at all, but leadership cults that drain the energy of their members and load them up with toxic stress. Because of this they are often factories of illness rather than centres of healing—*diabolical!*

We disciple the nations by demonstrating what the true social order, the true society, should be. This is more than individual discipleship, it is *community* discipleship, modelling a different kind of society and social order to the world so that the nations will turn to the Lord, as per Isaiah's prophecy: "And it shall come to pass in the last days, that the mountain of the Lord's house shall be established in the top of the mountains, and shall be exalted above the hills; and all nations shall flow unto it. And many people shall go and say, Come ye, and let us go up to the mountain of the Lord, to the house of the God of Jacob; and he will teach us of his ways, and we will walk in his paths: for out of Zion shall go forth the law, and the word of the Lord from Jerusalem. And he shall judge among the nations, and shall rebuke many people: and they shall beat their swords into plowshares, and their spears into pruninghooks: nation shall not lift up sword against nation, neither shall they learn war any more" (Isaiah 2:2–4).

We must disciple the nations by demonstrating what true society and true social order are, so that the nations will turn to God and learn this from us. This is how we disciple the nations: we are to incarnate the Kingdom of God in the way we live as Christian communities. The doctrine of the Trinity is important. The doctrine of the Trinity means the equal ultimacy of the one and the many. Individuals are important, and communities are important. One does not take precedence over the other. Both are equally important. But the Church today has abandoned this teaching for the priority of the individual.

We must be true Christian communities that model the Kingdom of God to the world as well as individual Christians that model the individual Christian life to the world. Otherwise we are no more than hermits. This societal aspect of the Christian life must be understood and practised. We must create Christian communities, Christian societies, if we are fulfil the Great Commission, which is a command to disciple *nations*.

§5
How to create Christian communities: Apostolic Foundations

We come now to the central question that I want to discuss, which is: How do we go about creating these Christian communities? The answer to this is that we need a catalyst around which a community can develop. To create a Christian community you need a core group of people with a shared vision and a sense of calling to the work that this vision requires for it to become a reality. In other words you need a core group of people with a shared *vision* and a sense of *mission* that can act as a focal point or catalyst around which a local community can form and develop, and from which missionaries can go out to other places to start the same process elsewhere.

How do we create these core groups that will initiate this process? For many Christians, indeed perhaps most, the obvious answer would seem to be the *Church*. The problem is that *this* answer does *not* work. Nor has it ever worked. There may have been isolated examples, but if so they are the exception, and do not constitute the general rule. The reason they do not work as a catalyst for the development of a Christian social order is that the Churches are obsessed with themselves and they almost inevitably end up as little more than Christian mystery cults and leadership cults, although *leadership* is probably the wrong word here, since they do not usually provided any real leadership in this respect at all. *Control cults* would be a better term. And the priority of the Churches is always on the ritualisation of the faith in the Church services, which of course, because they are deemed to be sacred rituals, have to be presided over by a priest, a mediator, who guards and validates the ritual. Of course this is a departure from the practice of the New Testament assemblies of believers and the Churches did not begin to develop along these lines until after the sub-apostolic age. But this development ultimately led to the restriction of the faith to the liturgical and the clerical. These things then became the be-all and end-all of the Christian faith. In other words the most important thing, the absolute focal point in the Christian life, becomes being a member of one of these cults and turning up for the regular ritual meetings in which the official magic is performed by the priest at the front. I am not referring here merely to the Episcopal Churches. This problem cuts across the whole spectrum of Church life, from the Episcopal Churches to the Free Churches and the Charismatic Churches. The rituals and the fancy dress differ between the various cults, i.e. the denominations, but the understanding of the faith is the same.

But the Church is not mean to be our focus. It is not what we are to seek before all else. The *Kingdom of God* and his *righteousness* are to be what we seek before all else. When we make the Church the focus of the faith we lose the Kingdom of God as a concrete reality. The Kingdom of God becomes almost indefinable in meaningful terms. If you doubt this try asking a Christian what the Kingdom of God is.

The biblical assemblies of Christians,—not the Church in the sense of a liturgical institution presided over by priests—are a *consequence* of our seeking the Kingdom of God and discipling the nations. In other words the Christian assemblies are a *consequence* of *apostolic mission*. Apostolic mission is what leads to the founding of the Christian assemblies. It is not the Church or the Christian assembly that leads to apostolic mission, but the other way round. Jesus told us that *he* would build his *ecclesia*, his assembly; he told *us* to seek first the Kingdom of God and disciple the nations. The leadership therefore comes from the apostolic missions, not the Churches. And the Christian communities and assemblies of Christians should follow and be led by the apostolic communities, the apostolic missions, upon which they are founded. But today this is the all the wrong way round, and it has been the wrong way round throughout much of Christian history. The Churches have become the leaders and the controllers of missions, which has really meant that they have usually acted as a brake on apostolic mission, and often they have been the wrecking ball of apostolic mission. This has been a disaster. Listen to what the apostle Paul says:

"For through him we both [i.e. Jews and Gentiles—SCP] have access by one Spirit unto the Father. Now therefore ye are no longer strangers and foreigners, but fellow citizens with the saints and of the household of God; and are built upon the foundation of the *apostles* and *prophets*, Jesus Christ himself being the chief corner stone" (Eph. 2:18:–20).

The Church today is *not* built upon the foundation of the apostles and prophets, but rather upon the foundation of *pastors* and *teachers*, something that is nowhere spoken of in the Bible, and this has been a disaster, a debacle. Pastors and teachers are not meant to be what the assemblies of Christians are founded on. The focus of the pastors and teachers is too narrow, and unfortunately usually totally obsessed with the Church cultus, which means ultimately that pastors and teachers are obsessed with themselves and their own celebrity status in the cult.

Pastors should be focused on those they are pastoring and teachers should be focused on teaching the word of God, but both are today primarily focused on themselves and the celebrity cults, big or small, that they call the Church. Leadership in the Great Commission and the seeking of the Kingdom of God is usually absent. The thing that matters is the cult, and the status of those who lead it. The whole of the Church meeting usually revolves around these leaders and they are the ones who do just about everything, or authorise an elite group of people to do things under their supervision, and effectively what this means is that the Christian's citizenship of the Kingdom of God is surreptitiously confiscated from him and vested in the clergy. This system is not found in the New Testament. In fact, it is contradicted by the practice of Christians in the New Testament. The Church as an institution has become a top-down authority structure, a hierarchy modelled on the kingdoms and power politics of the world. It was not this way in the New Testament. And the pastors and teachers have taken over as the ones who control ministry. But they are ill-equipped for this leadership, and nothing demonstrates this fact better than the deplorable state of the Churches under their leadership. They do have a role of course, that of pastoring and teaching, but often this gets lost in their desire to control not only all ministry in the Church, but the Church members as well, which they should not be doing, and often this gets very ugly. The focus of pastors and teachers is usually quite narrow, and they are very suspicious and obstructive of anyone with any apostolic vision for the expansion of the Kingdom of God. Primarily they function as the leaders of escapist cults, not leaders of world transforming apostolic missions. As a consequence, they are not suited to leadership of the body of Christ in its mission to disciple the nations and transform the world into the Kingdom of God. But in any case the assemblies of Christians should not be built on the foundation of the pastors and teachers, but on the foundation of the apostles and prophets. It was the *apostolic communities* that took the gospel around the world and founded the assemblies of Christians. And in the New Testament period it was the apostolic communities that provided the leadership. The apostolic community came first and the Christian assemblies were the result of their missions and followed their leadership.

The word of God has given us the correct order of things here, but the Church has ignored this and indeed actively opposed it. Unless we correct this error we shall not merely remain at the impasse we have reached, we shall go backwards, and indeed that is precisely what is happening. The body of Christ has gone as far as it possibly can go on this faulty and inverted model of leadership. The Church is on her knees before the world, and the Church leaders have no vision. Those with vision are constantly ostracised because they are perceived by the pastors and teachers as a threat to their own power base, but their "leadership" has led the Church and the world into the ditch: the blind leading the blind, as Jesus spoke of the Pharisees of his own day (Mt. 15:14).

The apostolic bands took the leadership in the New Testament age, and these were primarily itinerate. Today the Church, as an hierarchical institution, leads and controls the missions,—i.e. sends out and controls the missionaries. This is not the biblical order. In the Bible the apostolic community is in leadership. It is not controlled by the Churches. Rather, the assemblies of Christians are under the leadership of the apostolic community. The household of God is built on the foundation of the apostles and prophets, not on the foundation of the pastors and teachers, and we are now seeing where that faulty order has led us. The Church is in ruins today. She is a Church with no vision. The vision should be provided by the apostolic community. And because the Church has rejected this biblical order she has atrophied.

Now of course discussion of this whole subject has been made very difficult today by the Charismatic movement, which has done the faith and the world a great disservice by, among other things, adopting and championing a view of apostleship that is unbiblical and that is really no more than bishops by a different name, and bishops are part of the institutional Church edifice, not part of the apostolic communities or missions. There is nothing apostolic about bishops, whether in the Episcopal denominations or the Charismatic Churches. Apostles in these Churches are just jumped-up elders, bishops, who get to bully a group of Churches around instead of a single Church, and they work on the same theory of authority that the world has and that the Lord Jesus said was not to be how leadership worked in the Kingdom of God: "But Jesus called them unto him, and said, Ye know that the princes of the Gentiles exercise dominion over them, and they that are great exercise authority upon them. But it shall not be so among you: but whosoever will be great among you, let him be your minister; And whosoever will be chief among you, let him be your servant: Even as the Son of man came not to be ministered unto, but to minister, and to give his life a ransom for many" (Mt. 20:25–28).

It is commonly believed in many Churches, such as the older Free Church Protestant denominations, that the ministry of apostles ceased with the twelve apostles and Paul at the end of the New Testament age. But this idea is not derived from Scripture itself. The word *apostle* in the Greek means *one who is sent*, (*apostolos*, from the Greek verb *apostello*, meaning *to send*). This is the same word as *missionary* in English, which comes from the Latin verb *mitto*, meaning *to send*. *Apostle* and *missionary* mean the same thing. Of course those Churches that deny the continuing ministry of *apostles* beyond the New Testament age also assert the necessity and continuing validity of *missionaries*. But this makes no sense. How do apostles become valid and necessary just because we change the word by putting the concept into a different language? Missionaries are valid and necessary, but not apostles?—yet they mean exactly the same thing! The Bible nowhere sets forth the view that apostles were limited to the twelve disciples and the New Testament age. This idea has been read into the New Testament at best (*eisegesis*), and often not even that, but just asserted as ecclesial dogma. But because we have dispensed with a biblical category, we then need to reinvent it and give it another name, *missionary* or *bishop*—though the Episcopal use of the latter, *bishop*, involves just as much corruption of the biblical category as the Charismatic use of the word *apostle*. I do not of course subscribe to the modern hierarchical authoritarian idea of apostleship, either on the Charismatic or Episcopal understanding of the concept, neither of which I believe is biblical, and both of which I think have been read into Scripture. Jesus ruled out these authoritarian interpretations from the very beginning (Mt. 20:25–28). I understand why people would want to avoid talking about modern apostles. Most of those who like to use the term of themselves today, at least in the Church, are not apostles at all but are rather, like the bishops, merely tin-pot popes, i.e. authoritarian cult leaders. But it seems to me we cannot afford to dispense with biblical categories if we are going to understand Scripture properly. The answer therefore is not *non-use* but *correct* use of the term.

When I speak of apostolic communities and missions, therefore, I am not referring to the view of apostleship that prevails in the Charismatic Churches, which is not apostolic in any sense in my opinion. The apostolic communities are *not* power structures or hierarchies, they are communities with a vision for and a commitment to the Kingdom of God and the discipling of the *nations*, and with bringing all thought captive to and under the authority of the Lord Jesus Christ, and they are communities that are committed to this as their *mission*. These kinds of communities are sometimes referred to in missional language and by the Roman Catholic

Church as *sodalities*. The word *sodality* comes from a Latin word, *sodalitas*, which means *brotherhood*, *fellowship*, *a society* or *association*, and also *a company assembled for feasting*, or *banqueting club*, (in a bad sense it can mean *an unlawful secret society*).[32] These apostolic communities are not top-town hierarchies, but sodalities, communities of like-minded believers working together as brethren for the sake of the Kingdom and the conversion of the nations to the Christian faith across the whole spectrum of human life.

Well, if the Churches are not to be the catalyst around which the seeking of the Kingdom of God and the progress of the Great Commission are to revolve, what is? The answer is *apostolic communities*, *apostolic sodalities*. It is out of these that the creation of Christian communities will come and as a consequence of this we shall see the building up of the Kingdom of God and the discipling of the nations. And it has always been this way. The Christian communities and assemblies should therefore be apostolically led—but again, please note that I am not using the word *apostolic* in the Charismatic sense or the Episcopal sense. We need to reclaim the biblical language and terminology from those who have misused, abused and perverted it. We need to do this in order to understand Scripture properly and align ourselves with its teachings and priorities. The apostolic bands provided leadership in the New Testament. And despite the emergence of the Episcopal system—and by the way all Churches today are *functionally* Episcopal, regardless of any theory to the contrary—the apostolic communities or sodalities continued to lead the missions in the conversion of Europe. It was not the pastors and teachers that converted Europe, but the monasteries and monks, the *orders*, which were, despite all their problems, the heirs of the apostolic bands of the New Testament.

This leadership by the apostolic community requires centres of mission that can act as a catalyst for the development and growth of Christian communities and the growth of a Christian social order, out of which will come the discipling of the nations. This is how the early apostolic bands worked. This is what the monasteries were with all their problems. It is also what the early Protestant

[32] Lewis and Short, *op. cit.*, p. 1716*c*.

mission sodalities were. We need to establish apostolic communities that are leading the way across the whole spectrum of human life and forming communities that are *civilisations in seminal form.*

Setting up Churches has not and will not provide this leadership. Instead we need to create new sodalities, new centres of apostolic vision and mission, new communities committed and dedicated to the Kingdom of God as a counter-revolutionary prophetic social order governed by the covenant of grace that has come into this world now and is meant to grow until it displaces and eventually replaces the social orders of men. The assemblies of Christians are a result of this, not its cause, and as long as they follow the apostolic leadership they have an important role to play. If they reject the biblical model they will be blind guides leading the blind into the ditch, which is just what has happened.

There is a very interesting Jewish aphorism that goes like this: "The tail of the serpent said to the head, 'How much longer will you walk first? Let me go first' The head replied, 'Go.' The tail went and coming to a ditch of water dragged the head into it; it encountered a fire and pulled [the head into it]; and coming to thorns dragged it among them. What was the cause of all this? Because the head followed the tail. So when the rank and file follow the guidance of the leaders, the latter entreat God and He answers their prayers; but when the leaders permit themselves to be led by the rank and file, they perforce must share in the visitation that follows."[33] This is what has happened with the seeking of the Kingdom of God and the Great Commission. The Churches, i.e. the tail, have led the way and dragged the apostolic communities and missions, the head, into the ditch with them. This inverted order must be corrected if the Kingdom of God is to flourish and the Great Commission is to be fulfilled.

There is no one type or size fits all for these apostolic communities and centres of mission. There are a great many varieties and variables in this because there is a great variety of conditions in which they function. What will work in one place may not work in

[33] Midrash Rabbah, Vol. VII (Soncino Press, 1983), p. 9.

another and vice versa. But they will be Christian communities with this vision for the Kingdom of God and the Great Commission.

§6
Conclusion

We must create a Christian *social order*, a Christian *civilisation* in seminal form, out of which will come the conversion of the nations to the Lord Jesus Christ. The biblical term for this Christian social order, this Christian civilisation, is the *Kingdom of God*. It must grow until it displaces and eventually replaces the social orders, the civilisations, of men, and the Lord Jesus will not return until this has been accomplished. This vision for the kingdom of God and the Great Commission must be *apostolically* led. The assemblies of Christians are its fruit not its root, and therefore they must be grounded in the soil of *apostolic communities* with this vision for the Kingdom of God and the Great Commission.

In order to achieve this we need to establish and develop apostolic communities and ministries that are the modern-day successors of the monasteries and early Protestant sodalities. I am not proposing that we go back to the monasteries or the early Protestant sodalities as they were. We need to go far beyond these—forwards not backwards. But we need to learn from the past, both from the mistakes and the successes of the past. The monasteries were the heirs of the apostolic communities and bands of the apostolic and sub-apostolic age. We need to understand what the modern-day successors of these are, and we need to establish and develop such ministries, which will be as different from the monasteries as they are similar, for example, they will not be celibate or communistic, but they will be the manifestation of a completely different kind of social order from the social orders of the world, and they will be communities and ministries with a vision for and a commitment to seeking the Kingdom of God and the fulfilment of the Great Commission to make all the nations the disciples of the Lord Jesus Christ—i.e. to make Christian *nations*.

GENERAL INDEX